Suicide, Despair
and
Soul Recovery

Finding the Light of God

Ken Stifler

D1114328

Paulist Press
New York/Mahwah, NJ

The Scripture quotations contained herein are from the New Revised Standard Version: Catholic Edition Copyright © 1989 and 1993, by the Division of Christian Education of the National Council of the Churches of Christ in the United States of America. Used by permission. All rights reserved.

Quote appearing on p. 151 from *The Rumi Collection,* by Kabir Helminski, © 1998. Reprinted by arrangement with Shambhala Publications, Inc., www.shambhala.com

Poem by Kenneth Patchen on p. 131 from *Selected Poems* copyright © 1957 by Kenneth Patchen. Reprinted by permission of New Directions Publishing Corp.

Cover and book design by Lynn Else

Library of Congress Cataloging-in-Publication Data

Stifler, Ken.
    Suicide, despair and soul recovery : finding the light of God / Ken Stifler.
      p. cm.
    Includes bibliographical references.
    ISBN-13: 978-0-8091-4530-0 (alk. paper)
    1. Depression, Mental—Religious aspects—Christianity. 2. Suicide—Religious aspects—Christianity. 3. Depressed persons—Religious life. I. Title.
    BV4910.34.S75 2008
    248.8'628—dc22

2007052442

Published by Paulist Press
997 Macarthur Boulevard
Mahwah, New Jersey 07430

www.paulistpress.com

Printed and bound in the
United States of America

Contents

Affliction makes God appear to be absent for a time, more absent than a dead man, more absent than light in the utter darkness of a cell. A kind of horror submerges the whole soul. During this absence there is nothing to love. What is terrible is that if, in this darkness where there is nothing to love, the soul ceases to love, God's absence becomes final.

—Simone Weil

Foreword

As a pastoral counselor and spiritual director, I remember very well my twenty-four clients with issues of suicide. Seventeen are still with us, and seven "succeeded" in their efforts. Working with such troubled individuals causes enormous stress for a therapist. Several colleagues I know simply refuse to work with suicidal clients, and immediately refer them to others. Ken Stifler, however, has not flinched from courageously and compassionately assisting these wounded souls. In addition, he has written these wonderfully helpful reflections and suggestions, both for persons contemplating self-destruction, and for their counselors and concerned relatives or friends who may want to read and then pass on his book to others. With the author's permission, I have already sent my prepublication copy to one of my clients and she has informed me that this was immensely helpful to her.

The book is very personally written, deriving as it does from his years of experience working with suicidal persons. It contains concrete, practical suggestions about how such persons can reframe their gloomy thoughts, and what they can *do*.

Stifler begins with a good disclaimer: *A suicidal individual should always get professional help*. He then goes on to a crucial topic that many helping professionals avoid—spiritual issues. Stifler fills that lacuna with a book that is always spiritual, not "religious"; that is, it addresses humanity's highest, deepest values, and does not presume that the reader is a participant in any organized religious group.

The volume is addressed to "you"—"every person"—who is pondering suicide or who knows someone who is. The book is personal, even intimate, but *not* "folksy."

"Can a suicide be prevented?" asks one chapter, and Stifler responds with many good motives about the will to *live*. Simple, helpful analogies—like seeing a dentist if "you" have a toothache, or trusting the wind again after a shipwreck of "your" boat—create in the client a willingness to be helped by others.

The chapter on "Understanding the Suicidal Condition" reviews the story of Ernest Hemingway's final days and helps one get "inside" the mind and heart of anyone contemplating causing one's own end. Stifler provides other such narratives, as well as poems and quotations from both the East and West, each concerning the ultimate meaning of life, even a life of pain and suffering.

In the chapter "Damage Control," he wisely counsels *waiting* for a solution to occur, and mirrors Jung's aphorism, *"Omnis festinatio a diabolo est,"*; that is, *"All haste derives from the devil."* He reminds us of the Chinese puzzle that we played with as children: the straw tube we put on a finger of opposing hands, our own or a friend's, and then tried to pull the hands apart. It's impossible because we tried too hard. We had to relax into a solution, just as with suicidal ruminations.

In "The Role of Adversity," he suggests remembering that anything less than God (or one's "Higher Power") fails to satisfy. *Reframing* changes our perspective: a flat tire saved us from an accident ahead on the road; the butterfly changes into a caterpillar. Suffering ultimately can lead to growth. The chapter "Live the Questions" helps unpack the conundrums filling the mind of a depressed, despairing person. "Soul Recovery" points to the secret center of the world found within the core of everyone.

The chapter "Going to God" concludes the book and "refers" one to the ultimate "helping professional."

In summary, Ken Stifler has written a book that should be placed in the hands of anyone suffering the torment of suicidal intentions, as well on the shelf of any professional assisting family members of clients seeking this "way to end it."

William Sneck, SJ, PhD
Jesuit Center for Spiritual Growth
Wernersville, Pennsylvania

*This book is lovingly dedicated to my mother,
Dorothy Virginia Stifler,
who has taught me, more than any other saint,
that love is the meaning of life.*

Disclaimer

This book offers a "psycho-spiritual" approach to the problems of suicide and despair. The spiritual principles implicit in this presentation, however, are in no way meant to replace or discourage adequate psychiatric care. Research has consistently demonstrated that medication and psychotherapy are effective means of treatment, and the suicidal person should never abandon medical or psychological care in order to pursue purely religious or spiritual methods. Of the hundreds of suicidal persons I have worked with over the past thirty years, the majority of them have desperately needed medication and counseling, in addition to spiritual care.

In this course of this book the importance of soul recovery and renewal will be emphasized without disparaging or minimizing the importance of medications, psychiatric hospitalizations, mental health counseling or any other "secular" or "medical" approaches. At the outset do not attempt to try and manage any seriously suicidal condition, be it your own or that of one you love, without the help of the professional psychiatric community.

It would not be wise to advise a person with a broken arm to forget about a cast but to pray or memorize some sacred scripture verse instead. Telling a suicidal person to examine one's soul but to forgo medication or counseling would be just as unwise. God uses doctors, therapists, social workers and medications to accomplish his work.

If at this moment you or someone whom you know poses an imminent danger to the self, you must take immediate and appropriate action. Call 911, or get yourself to the nearest emergency department or mental health clinic. Remove any lethal weapons or means of self-harm if possible, and make a decision right now to seek help without wasting any more precious time. You must seek immediate physical intervention and safety.

This book is not a mental health emergency intervention kit or an acute crisis protocol. The presence of suicidal thoughts or plans is enough to confirm that the condition has already progressed beyond what a book of this sort can offer. Professional attention is needed right away. You can contact local police or call 1-800-suicide or 1-800-784-2433 for the National Hopeline Network. There are knowledgeable and caring people in your community who can and will respond. You do not need to have transportation, money or insurance to get this help.

Although this book is not for the imminently suicidal, it is for anyone who has recently survived a suicide attempt or has been contemplating one but does not presently have an immediate plan or intent to complete the act. Likewise, it is intended for the persons who recognize in themselves the presence of a suicidal attitude or frame of mind: people who no longer care to live, who passively wish for a sudden or accidental death or have given up on themselves or life in general. It is for anyone in despair or for anyone who is merely interested in the topic or in need of a little inspiration. This book is also a useful tool for anyone looking for something to offer a family member, friend or loved one who may be battling despair or bobbing in the stormy seas that follow in the wake of a suicide attempt or gesture. Professionals in the helping arts—therapists, pastors, chaplains, social workers, teachers, nurses and others—may benefit as well.

So, if you are safe from immediate danger and have reason to believe you can benefit, please read on.

INTRODUCTION
Before the Flooding Brink

Approximately thirty thousand people commit suicide every year in this country alone,[1] and nearly a million kill themselves worldwide annually.[2] An estimated five hundred thousand more receive attention in hospital emergency departments for suicide attempts here in America alone.[3] There are hundreds of thousands more who are never counted: deaths that are wrongly determined to be "accidental," attempts that go untreated, suicides that are covered over for politeness, political correctness or insurance purposes. Perhaps many millions have been touched by suicide directly or indirectly.

If you consider that we are also committing a form of intellectual, emotional or spiritual "suicide" every time we give up, surrender to addiction and despondency, turn against our self, reject happiness, withdraw our affections and attentions from life, despise God, alienate our loved ones, undermine our future, wallow in self-pity, attach ourselves to negativity, refuse to move on from the past, hurt others, block our successes or curse the day we were born, then you will begin to think as I do about suicidal despair. Everyone is affected in one way or another.

When you think of the thousands upon thousands more who are family members and friends to these suicidal individuals, and the thousands more who become involved with them through providing emergency services, funerals, treatment and other forms of outreach, you will recognize that the entire world is touched by suicide.

1

Some Examples

I have been personally involved for as long as I can remember. I used to play tennis with a dentist who apologized after every shot. He was an exceedingly nice person. Another was a friend who introduced me to Black Sabbath in junior high school and enjoyed causing a stir, like the time we exploded homemade wine all over his parents' fancy white walls. A psychiatrist friend of mine thought he was a reincarnated Civil War hero; he was a very eccentric but brilliant individual. My wife's cousin was one of the nicest people you could ever meet, but he never seemed to stop wringing his hands. A counselor apprentice that I supervised was a prep school Greek teacher who restored classic cars. Another teenage boy whom I placed into a foster care home, an incredibly handsome and talented young man, would get on my nerves by banging too hard on my guitar and riding his skateboard through my house. Then there was the wealthy businessman who seemed to make the quickest and most remarkable recovery I had ever seen in a psychiatric hospital anywhere when we sent him out on a weekend pass.

Every one of these individuals is now dead by suicide, brutally murdered by their own hands. They died by gunshot wounds, lethal overdoses, hangings and carbon dioxide poisoning. I liked them all, and I miss them now. However, there was nothing anyone could have done to predict or prevent these suicides because every one of these people kept their plans of self-destruction to themselves. Although every one of these deaths could have been prevented, not one of these people allowed anyone in their inner lives. All of them secretly schemed and planned their deaths, then without warning, in solitude and despair, thinking there was no other option, took their own lives. Something could have been done. However, they never asked, never talked nor allowed themselves to be helped.

Preventing Suicide

I remember the first time I ever tried to prevent a suicide. I was sixteen years old, and a seeming confused young girl everyone called "crazy Sue" used to telephone me late summer nights to tell me about her plans to cut her wrists or take pills. I would try to talk her out of killing herself. Perhaps she was not all that serious. Maybe she was just flirting with the idea or using her feminine wiles to captivate my attention, but she had tried it a couple times before, and without me there, she would have been all alone with these thoughts. She never tried suicide again during that period, and I do think my presence had something to do with that. Maybe it was something entirely different, but I was glad to be a small part of whatever that was. It seemed important, and still does today. People who are all alone with their despair carry twice the weight of it with half the strength, and are frequently overcome with these thoughts.

My being there for her helped me as well. To be invited into such an inner personal space between one's desire to die and their "seeking in the dark" for a reason to go on made me feel as if my life had some meaning. That experience was one of many that helped lead me into a career that I now accept as part of my destiny.

The next suicidal individual to cross my path was a man with whom I roomed the following year. He had a bullet hole in his chest from a suicide attempt gone awry. Although I felt sorry for him, he no longer felt sorry for himself. He said that he had found God and was a completely changed man. He was happy and believed God kept him alive despite the shooting, because he said he had aimed very carefully at his heart and did not think it possible to have missed his target, and, unbelievably, to have survived.

Not long after that time, I met a dozen suicidal people who were involuntarily committed to a big concrete psychiatric institution in Bangor, Maine. As a young chaplain intern there, I tried to tell them about God. Many of them assured me that their lives were proof that there is no God. One said that his .44 caliber magnum was his god. Another said he worshiped Satan as his god.

Some Observations

Since then I have met hundreds more individuals, among them suicidal children, adults and the elderly. Some were near geniuses, others mentally deficient. Many were beautiful, rich and strong; others sick, poor and weak. Some were psychotically ill, but others were professionally trained and impeccably sane. Some were quite religious while others seemed to have no faith at all. Some had experienced profound suffering and loss, while others were upset over minor irritations. I have seen them in Florida, Maryland, Virginia, Maine and Minnesota, in private swanky hospitals, backward state institutions, jails, outpatient counseling centers, drug rehab clinics, social work offices and college guidance departments. They were white, black, red and brown. Some had horrible scars on their wrists, necks and chests, and every one, without exception, had scars on their hearts.

Some had tried suicide over ten or twenty times while others had thought about it most of their lives but had not yet acted on it. Some I had talked to just minutes before their suicide attempt, others right after they were cut down from a noose or pulled from a car rigged up like a gas chamber. Some were deadly serious and others seemed to be fooling around or asking for help. Many had thrown themselves in front of trains and trucks, drank poison, exploded guns in their faces, jumped from bridges, taped plastic bags around their heads, shoved knives into their chests, electrocuted themselves and more. Some were almost humorous, like the woman who tried to drown herself in a sink or the diabetic who ate a box of Twinkies and threatened to eat another to do herself in.

However, there is nothing funny about wanting to kill yourself. I have taken every situation very seriously. Some I helped while others slipped through the cracks. On most occasions, I just did whatever I could—nothing exceptional, heroic or unusual given my position. As a mental health professional, I have depended on the theories and techniques of psychology and medicine. I have taken detailed social histories, documented stressors, uncovered hidden traumas, confronted addictions, battled resistances, had people hospitalized and locked in padded rooms, chased them down the street, talked them down on the phone and rushed to get them a shot of a tranquilizer.

As a self-appointed minister of sorts, I have prayed for all of them. For the most part, I have stopped talking about God a long time ago, because I have been forced to do this. Supervisors, administrators and "clinical protocol," as it is generally accepted, typically suggest it is intrusive, preachy, unethical and beyond one's clinical identity and boundaries to delve into religion. They say people do not want to hear about spiritual matters especially when they are in crisis. There appears to be some truth in that observation. No one wants a moralizer, preacher or prayer warrior jumping in her face when she is being terrorized by misfortune.

The Need for the Spiritual

Yet, this attitude is reactive and one-sided, a sort of overkill born of professional blindness and a prejudicial smugness that assumes "scientific" knowledge is superior to faith, that the head contains information superior to the heart and that a person's soul is disembodied from his psychological conflict. This attitude cheats the client of the possibility of receiving a full-spectrum intervention. Many suicidal people want to talk about God. They have questions about the morality of their choice, concerns about the afterlife, unsettled thoughts about the consequences of a self-inflicted death, hopes of going to a better place or being with loved ones and ongoing doubts and debates about the justice and availability of God in times of trouble. Many, in fact, who have had serious suicidal thoughts have refrained from acting on them *only* because they have been concerned with the afterlife implications. In my experience, this concern has kept more people from killing themselves than any other.

Although it is certainly inappropriate for a clinician to try to convert others or to push one's own personal agenda, it is equally inappropriate to ignore or dismiss the client's spiritual concerns. It might even be considered unethical to keep certain known effective antisuicidal strategies, such as faith, hope and love, from the people who most need them. Suicidal clients are far more than clinical "conditions" with psychiatric labels that fit squarely into our diagnostic categories and treatment protocols. These are people with spiritual histories, crises of faith, loss of meaning, faltering hope, isolation from community, questions of guilt, moral dilemmas and a need for the depths of existential meaning and unconditional love. Like all of us, they wrestle with God every day. Some do this more consciously than others. To be alive means to query the purpose of life, to contemplate fate, to question death, to wonder at the mysteries and uncertainties that perplex every living and breathing human on a daily basis.

Although the efficacy of medication and psychotherapy is very clear, we must never lose sight of the fact that suicide, the hopelessness and despair that accompany it, the helplessness and desperation that lead to it, the attendant guilt and self-loathing, the choice to destroy or save a human life are all sacred concerns. This crisis has everything to do with faith, hope, love and the condition of one's soul. These "spiritual concerns" are no more important than the physical, mental or social concerns, but they are equal and must be given equal emphasis and the opportunity to be explored.

Some think they have no spiritual concerns. Others are not ready to be helped by any means, spiritual or otherwise. In addition, there are administrative constraints on clinicians, situational factors and limitations on how well prepared certain crisis workers are to address such things. The tone of the discussion, the place, context and timing must all be just right.

Even you, now, as you are reading this, may not be completely ready to accept a spiritual approach. However, if you need help with suicidal thinking, know someone else who does or have the least bit of interest in seeing God involved in the healing of that condition, then you are already being drawn to this by God. It is impossible to concern ourselves with God unless God is "stirring us up." If you are sensing a stir, it means that grace is already at work. Grace first appears as a nagging interest in faith, or a memory of some past experiences with God. Sometimes it crops up as a "coincidence," in which we find ourselves falling into the lap of spiritually charged information. So here you are.

If you think that perhaps now could be the time to concern yourself with the health of your soul, then that thought, curiosity, willingness, questioning or longing is a sure sign that it is time. Grace is already calling your name.

Some Hopes

This presentation attempts to explore what God has to do with suicide and despair in general. I have attempted a format that makes this discussion easy for you to take or leave as you wish. I will not try to tell you how you should understand God but recommend you think of him in terms that make the most sense to you. More important, I encourage you to ask God to reveal himself to you as he is in truth. Although I use the masculine gender and the term *God* in reference to this divine reality, I recognize that this reality cannot be adequately defined or contained in any one particular name or gender.

I have asked myself what role grace, faith and God might play in the healing of suicidal conditions and what the saints and mystics offer on this topic. I've questioned why or how a person loses hope, how it might be regained, where one without any source of help might begin to find divine guidance and support and how religious literature might explain unexplainable suffering. I have not come to any absolute conclusions. Some of the questions raised opened further questions. These reflections are offered as a way of encouraging you to wrestle with the same questions, not because you will figure them out but because in the wrestling you will have found your way. To the suicidal person, there is nothing more important than this.

The rest of this book will not be so much about statistics or my personal experiences. A few of these observations are mentioned at the outset just so that you will know you are not alone and that you might have a little confidence in what I am about to say. My interest is not to impress you with my credentials or with the number of suicidal individuals whom I have tended. Admittedly, I am just as baffled by suicide as most people are. Even the experts in this line of work are still basically confused and baffled by this social phenomenon.

We cannot accurately predict who will commit suicide nor can we guarantee which treatments will work. No one is really certain why some people become suicidal while others in a similar predicament become determined to overcome their obstacles. Suicidal behavior is a very individualistic thing. It cannot be controlled, predicted or eradicated by science.

I am not trying to offer here some new research, nor am I interested in adding another book for the academic or clinical expert. My intention is to try to help the suicidal person, to plant seeds of love, hope and faith. My appeal is based purely on a belief that there is hope, that life is good as it is, that everyone is worthy of being happy and that it is possible for people to find freedom from suffering. I have no doubt that God is an active and present force in all of our lives and that there is an undisclosed meaning behind all the apparent meaninglessness and chaos in the world.

God is an adventure, an incomprehensible mystery that we are each, in our own unique way, called to enter. God's activity in the world is a bit like falling in love or laughing at a funny joke. You must experience it and taste it for yourself. It is also like beauty or poetry, available and calling out for our attention and appreciation at every instant, yet so easily ignored or missed because of the drama and pain and confusion that threaten to keep us off balance and focused elsewhere for the majority of our lives.

I am convinced that the worst of times is meant for our good and that even the most chaotic and unfair tragedies hold a hidden meaning. I have learned that when we think we cannot go on, we can, and that when we run out of our own strength and hope we can borrow some from others. I am certain that everyone can find a measure of truth and meaning and that everyone deserves another chance. I have never seen a hopeless case. Every desperate, confused, weak or torn soul is being equipped and made ready for the advent of grace. In fact, it may be true that, just as the alcoholic has to "bottom out" before he can loosen his attachment to the bottle, so the self-assured, controlled, satisfied and contented individual who is overly "dependent" on ego may have to come to the end of her strength in order to let go of her ego addiction and allow God in.

It is most helpful for the despairing person to recognize that wounds are messengers, troubles are teachers, failures are guides and heartache is not the end of the world. We are being called to let go, to live in God and to realize our true selves. We may never be able to do any of this without the push that trouble gives.

This is soul work, and in working the soul, it may help to recall that Jesus said there is no profit to be gained, even if one gains the whole world, if the soul is lost.[4] Conversely, we can assume the loss of the world to be a very small thing if in the process the soul is found. Soul means everything, for without soul, all else is meaningless.

CHAPTER 1
Darkness in the Heart

It seems clear to me that stabbing yourself, cutting your wrists, burning your body, drowning or suffocating yourself, shooting yourself, taking a lethal overdose, drinking poison, inhaling gas, throwing yourself from a bridge or hanging yourself are negative manifestations of the darkness that is in the world. This is not to say that people beset with such thoughts or actions are evil but, rather, that a great darkness has come upon them.

Darkness pervades the interior landscape of anyone who is void of hope and overwhelmed with negativity and despair. Self-hatred, murderous intent and destructive hopelessness are dark forces indeed. Darkness is a fitting metaphor for suicide, the death instinct, the dark night of the soul and despair. By contrast, light is a telling metaphor for love, joy, hope, faith and wisdom. The things that give us meaning or cause us to feel compassion, creativity or happiness, the innocence of a child, the love of another, the fresh buds of spring, a mother's touch or a father's strong support can be easily seen as "lights" or light-producing energies. Light makes us happy, content and full. It chases away the "blues," or darker shades of mood, causing one to grow or heal, to be illuminated, free of anxiety and fear.

Although darkness can seem intimidating, it really has very little power, especially against the force of light. Whenever light is introduced into a darkened area, the light dominates. Even if it is a very small light, the dark cannot successfully keep it out. The dark can do nothing to resist or overtake the light. Once light arrives, darkness recedes, and everything the light touches is transformed. That which appeared to be black and formless in the dark is revealed to be full of color and texture, and its interesting shapes and sizes are made apparent by the light. The dull impenetrable void becomes vibrant and alive through the presence of light, and in just this same way a darkened heart can become alive again in the presence of the light of love, wisdom and hope.

Dispelling Darkness

The only way to dispel darkness, be it metaphorical or real, is to introduce light. It is impossible to fight against darkness by a force of will, intelligence or skill. We cannot beat it off with a stick, wish it to go away or pretend it is not there. The best thing to do, perhaps the only thing we can do, is to turn on a light or else wait for the coming of the light of the morning sun.

Darkness can occur either naturally or by a willful interference with light. Sometimes our life goes dark through a natural course of events. Darkness descends without our consent, like the coming of winter or night, over which we have no control. We did not produce it nor can we make it go away. This is similar to what occurs when one is stricken with cancer or is faced with the death of a loved one. We can only wait it out and look for an alternate source of light. There are other times, however, when we produce or encourage the darkness through ignorance, aversion and attachment. This is when we diminish the light within willfully through our stupidity, anger, passion, selfishness or greed. In these instances, we can do something more immediate and proactive to dispel the dark.

In cases of suicidal despair, we often find people who have either "caused" or allowed the darkness to dominate. Although this is frequently accomplished without our conscious awareness, it is still something that we perpetuate through voluntary participation or tacit consent and can be dispelled through proactive initiation of the light. This is not to place blame but to empower you. You can forgive yourself, and the light of that love can dispel the darkness of your despair. We can make peace with God, and that peace can replace our unrest.

There are many ways that we block the light, but the primary way is through a blocking of the light within us, the original light of the true self, which attempts to make manifest the divine spark of hope and love that has been seeded within. The true self is its own kind of light, but it is also an aperture through which we receive the manifestations of the infinite light of divine love, beauty, wisdom and hope. We interfere with this opening in the self every time we allow our hearts to become restricted, hard or shut down. We close our hearts and block its light through self-hatred, self-rejection, repression of feelings, denial of the past, attachment to the past, fear of the future or resistance to our present reality and ourselves. Light is extinguished from our hearts every time we despise our weaknesses, ridicule our dreams or refuse to forgive ourselves for our failures. It is made dark inside us every time we reject or spoil the light of love from others or from God. The darkness is intensified with every act of deceit, hatred, greed or selfishness. We close our hearts with every fear and regret, and everything goes black inside us when we lose touch with our self, the truth, hope or love.

Seeing the Light Within

The true "self," or light within us, can be shut off in many ways. Others may abuse, reject or ridicule us, and we can "take it to heart," allowing these things to harden or diminish our capacity for illumination, openness, gentleness and authenticity. We also weaken this light every time we practice cruelty, criticism or rejection of ourselves or others for the mistakes and imperfections we all make. But the darkness really deepens when we willingly betray our true self in order to please or impress others. Even God does not want that of us. By bruising our innocence and wonder, abandoning our inner life, destroying our innate capacity for love and allowing others to intimidate us out of ourselves, we diminish the light within and surrender our true destiny and birthright, which is to live fully.

All of us have been reinforced to belittle and batter the aspects of who we are. Many of us have been shamed or told we are not good enough by parents or teachers. Males may be told they should not be too sensitive. Females often risk rejection if they are perceived as being too tough. Children are told to grow up, and older adults are expected to look and act younger than they are. Many people find that their cultural ways are scorned, dreamers and artists are often unappreciated, people with faults are called sinners, gays are tormented, country folks are called rednecks, overweight people are treated like lepers and intellectuals are taunted as geeks. Self-righteous religionists try to condemn us for overeating or sleeping in on Sunday.

In this seemingly aggressive and competitive world, it is sometimes very difficult to be who and what we are and to love ourselves for it. Society places its primary value on surface appearances, conformity and external measures of success. It judges, compares and rejects people for simply being who they are on the visible outside. To most of the world, it does not matter what you really are inside. Others want you to please them and support their way of thinking and behaving. You are to keep your dreams to yourself, especially if they are different or do not fit the current model for what is seen as "cool." The "inner you," your true heart, that unrelenting core of sanity that was created to love and to celebrate living, to discover and make beautiful things, that central, still and quiet center in your heart of hearts is where the light begins. To recover that is the recovery of soul.

The death, repression or loss of our true self precedes the later deaths we inflict upon ourselves by suicide, despair or self-neglect. The latter are just easier to see.

This loss of self is no small thing. It is always lurking about at the core of every significant depression or state of despair. The capacity to realize and honor one's most authentic inner being is the foundation for any lasting happiness, realization or enlightenment. Thus, if you observe within yourself any depth of unhappiness, uncertainty or lack of meaning, you can be certain it has something to do with your failure to appreciate, understand and accept your own depths.

Darkness in one's life comes about in many ways. It may be the result of a genuinely pervasive night, such as the loss of a loved one or a serious medical condition, or it may be related to the loss of self. There may be other contributing factors as well, but the point is, in any case, to identify the reason for the darkness and to figure out how it may be dispelled.

The Soul's Light

The word *dispel* is most appropriate when talking about ridding one's self of the dark because darkness casts a kind of spell. It disenchants the once enchanted person and covers her eyes with scales. Darkness disorients and confuses even the most capable, making it impossible for them to see things as they are, no matter how hard they try. In the dark we lose our way, expect the worst, believe in negativity, chase illusions and fear the trembling movement beneath our bed. It is difficult to see things in any other way. We trip over things we once easily avoided. As its mystifying presence bewitches us and clouds our perceptions, we can soon forget that there is light and another world entirely.

To restore the soul and reilluminate the light within us, we must examine our hearts and find out how we may have tarnished our original brilliance or allowed other people and things to do the same. We may discover ways to limit or eradicate the level of darkness we have allowed to enter us, to reduce our dark-inducing habits, perceptions and practices and to learn how to become reacquainted with the light of our true being. We may need to learn how to let other people's drama and the disappointments of daily life to flow off our backs. We may need to reestablish a relationship with the divine, the source and sole originator of all light. We will have to fall in love and become lovers. We may need to learn how to wait in patience for the sun to rise or the winter to pass. All of these things are important in considering how to negotiate our way back to the light.

The ancient Greeks referred to this inner light or true self as our *daemon*, the in-spirited, creative and life-giving core that was bestowed upon each of us by the gods at birth in order to establish wholeness, equanimity and balance in our lives and to direct us in discovering the meaning and purpose of our time here on earth. Buddhists refer to this as our original face or Buddha nature and claim that by returning to the *One True Self*, one is awakened to the truth of freedom from suffering through its wisdom and selfless compassion. Hindus speak of the *One True Self* that is hidden in the lotus of the heart. Muslim mystics speak of the same light within, as do Taoists. Jewish masters of the Hasidic and Kabalistic traditions teach the same, as do most Shamanic and Native American spiritualities. Christians speak of the body as being the temple of the Holy Spirit and recognize the inner light of love as Christ in us, the hope of glory.

The light that dispels the darkness is already within us. If we are not realizing it or benefiting from its manifest brilliance, we are being challenged to find out why and to discover just how we might reacquaint ourselves with its flame.

This light that we seek and need is more than the light of human reason or affections, for it is the divine spark of God within us. Yet divinity also shines in the simplest mundane pleasures and human affections. Divinity is breached both within and beyond the mundane particulars of our lives and our human interactions. Jesus is considered to have been the manifest image of the Godhead in bodily form. We will do well to remember that it was *in his bodily form* that he was divine, not in some otherworldly pure spirit. By reacquainting ourselves with our deepest humanity, we reach into that place where God reaches into us. If we are ever going to reach God, we will have to do so through our human self in the very real relationships and tragedies we encounter day to day. There is no shortcut to this mystery by becoming "spiritually" enlightened without also becoming an authentic human being. Nor is it possible to simply become a fully realized human person without reaping the benefits of the presence and participation of divine grace.

Here is where the soul does its work. It bridges the gap between the human and divine, integrating the sacred and profane, uniting the gulf between grace and works, making sense of our aloneness and simultaneous participation in the all. Soul strives to show us our acceptability in being exactly who we are in all our brilliance and dullness, ugliness and beauty, passion and indifference, and in doing so it heals us of the tragic turning against ourselves that is characteristic of all suicidal despair.

Soul strives to orchestrate the multilayered complexity of our humanly divine lives, mixing light and dark, pleasure and pain, clarity and confusion, love and indifference all into a collective masterpiece. Like the master works of Mozart, movement and silence and repetition are masterfully blended to produce a coherent whole, neither ignoring nor exaggerating the variations that make for things as they are, but placing them all into a balanced contextual arrangement that uses every part to illuminate the whole.

Life remains the same following the illumination of soul as it was before, with good days and bad, sickness and health, heartaches and joys, winnings and losses, but with this one difference: love sanctifies and unifies it all. In love one's burdens are lighter, the path is brighter, everything makes more sense and there is reason to go on.

When the light in one's soul becomes dulled, neglected or abused, the inspiration for living is thwarted and provides an opportunity for the destructive, life-denying forces of darkness to take over our consciousness, will and emotional life. We become "un-inspirited," hollowed out and lifeless.

Very few of us ever figure out how to trust in the light all the time. There are so many obstructions within and without. We lose touch, we turn against ourselves, we become angry and bitter with others, we go through tough times, we worry and we wonder about the fairness or even the reality of God. Even in the best of times we are all too aware of the contingency, fragility and terminal nature of our lives. There will always be moments of grief and sadness. Even Jesus wept.

If we are not careful, this world's sorrow, our ignorant and wandering ways, the lure of dark pleasures and our own need to punish ourselves or run from who we actually are will drain us of the light. Before we know it, the inspiration of God's Spirit that once filled us with the vigorous life-enhancing and creative momentum we enjoyed as children can be lost. We can be left only with lethargy, ill will, hopelessness and despair. The darkness that we seek to dispel is this bitter, negativistic, pessimistic, grave, inauthentic, shallow and listless experience. The light we seek, and that which is seeking us, is the light of love.

This diminishment of one's life force, the deadening of the will to live, love and create is mostly considered to be a medical malady these days, but in Jesus' time it was commonly considered a spiritual problem. He drove out the darkness and was constantly calling for renewal, a turning away from the ways of hatred, self-interest and doubt so that his hearers might be born again "of the Spirit" and baptized into the light. He invited everyone who had lost their inspiration to be regenerated and renewed in heart and soul, so that the Spirit of God might freely flow into their being, ushering them into the kingdom of God, making known to them a God who is Father and Friend, promising fruits of love, joy, peace, gentleness, goodness, meekness, temperance and faith.[1] According to Jesus, drinking of the waters of his life, the path of love, was the way to happiness, the truth of being and the refreshment that satisfied completely without end.

Today the use of medications and psychotherapy are the prevailing methods for dealing with despair and the loss of the will to live. However, we have become overly fixated on treating only the mind and body, having neglected the soul. There is nothing wrong in the former but it is a grave mistake to forget the latter. If we are to deal effectively with the forces of darkness and despair, we cannot forget what Jesus said or ignore, for that matter, what every other authentic spiritual master down through the ages has taught us about this.

For thousands of years people believed in dispelling the darkness of despair through prayer, repentance, holy living, community involvement, meditation, sacred reading, practices of selfless service and ritual. Not every one of these practices has been helpful, and religion has certainly done much at times to alienate people from themselves and to induce guilt and despair. However, for the most part, the true nature of authentic spirituality has done more to dispel depression, madness and despair than science, medicine, philosophy or psychology has ever done or can ever hope to do. The beauty is that, now in this enlightened age, we do not have to choose one over the other. We can take our Prozac in the morning and still pray our way through the day.

The Threshold to a New Life

Furthermore, I see an important parallel between the giving up or surrendering of one's life that characterizes the suicidal person's position and the surrendering of one's self that is required for spiritual transformation. The saint and the suicidal person both find something repulsive in the ego-centered self, the world's illusory promises and the failures and imperfections they have endured. It seems to be a small leap of faith that separates one from the other.

Edward Hoagland makes an interesting observation. He said, "Suicidal thinking, if serious, can be a kind of death scare, comparable to suffering a heart attack or undergoing a cancer operation. One survives such a phase both warier and chastened. When—years ago—I emerged from a bad dip into suicidal speculation, I felt utterly exhausted and yet quite free of ordinary dangers, vastly afraid of myself but much less scared of extraneous eventualities."[2]

The suicidal person stands on the threshold between this world and the world beyond, between abandonment to the abyss and abandonment to God. The ego has exhausted all its resources, and surrender may be its only option. The person in that position is being asked to consider whether one should surrender to defeat or to a greater meaning. Also, there are gradients between, and a person has the option of refusing to surrender at all and returning to the life lived prior to despair, the one that led him to despair in the first place. These choices are of great consequence.

Facing suicidal despair is akin to "suffering a heart attack or undergoing a cancer operation." It forces one to face the most critical questions of meaning, of being and existence at the deepest levels.

Imagine a ninety-four-year-old man with terminal cancer but a clear mind lying on his bed awaiting the angel of death. In those final hours he will think about the meaning of his life. Maybe the angel of death himself will pose the questions, but this will be a time when the circumstances will force him to reflect and give an accounting of his life. He may ask himself, "What have I done with my life? Have I made a difference? Did I do everything I could to tap my fullest potential, or did I waste the years? Have I loved? Do I have any regrets?"

The suicidal person crosses this threshold as well, and with death posing as such a viable and potential threat, is forced to ask herself, "What does my life mean?" She may find it means very little or that she has made a mess of things, but now, having either survived a suicide attempt or outlived the temptation to die, she is left with the option and opportunity to do something about what she has seen.

This crisis of meaning in the face of death is brilliantly portrayed in the movie based on Chuck Palahniuk's book *Fight Club*. In one scene the main character holds a gun to the head of a young convenience store clerk and demands to know why he has abandoned his efforts to become a veterinarian. In a psycho-horror sort of way this gunman is a vigilante for the meaning of life. He believes he is doing the clerk a favor by forcing him to face death, then offering him his life back on the condition that he reclaim his heart. He gives him ten weeks to reenroll in college or he will be killed. This madman's message is wisdom, albeit wrapped in insanity.[3]

We must not allow our trivial fears and concerns to put us off track of our life's meaning. It is noble and respectable to work with your hands, shovel coal, sweep floors, program computers—whatever it is you do. Just be careful not to rot there and shrivel away if you know there is more in you. Don't sell your soul to please others, gain some vested retirement or pursue a false sense of security. Remember your heart. Reclaim the light. We don't have to face suicidal despair or a life-threatening illness before we remember ourselves, but it helps.

Another scene in the movie version of *Fight Club* is worthy of mention. In this scene our desperado of meaning is speeding his car down a crowded freeway. He releases his hold on the steering wheel in a sort of Russian roulette game with oncoming traffic and asks the two passengers in the backseat what they wished they could accomplish before they die. One says he always wanted to paint a self-portrait, the other to build a house. If you have ever been suicidal, you have been on this ride and have had the gun pressed against your head.

Now you are asked to answer these questions about your meaning. What are the things you have left undone? What do you regret? When will you return to your heart? Finding your way back to yourself does not have to involve a major change, like reenrolling in medical school. It may be something as small as walking barefoot in the grass or daring to wear purple more often, as the well-known poem states.

This crisis of meaning, the crossroad between living and dying, is where the suicidal person is ripe for soul renewal. This renewal may mean making things right with a loved one, writing a book, dancing in the streets or joining a prayer group. Whatever it is, if it is a choice for life over death, it is the beginning of a journey back to the self that will ultimately lead one back to the reality of God. It is the beginning of allowing the light to once again dispel the dark.

The only dark place that cannot be illuminated is the darkened room that we lock ourselves into when we refuse to open the door.

We are all invited, every day, to open the door. We are being challenged to allow in more light than dark. We are also being asked to send out more light than dark. We are not being unreasonably asked to create this light through hard labor, but are rather empowered to choose it freely from the unlimited source within.

CHAPTER 2
Wounded Innocence

You are wounded, not deformed. Before you ever thought about losing hope, giving up, contemplating suicide or turning against yourself in any way, you were happy, blissfully alive and content. You may not even be able to recall it now, but this is your original condition. It is the birthright of every person. We are born in innocence and wonder. We are born to be happily engaged in all of life, to love and be loved, to grow and laugh, to explore our world, to create and take risks, to lose our way and find it again, to rise and fall, to reap and sow, to care about others and to hope and dream. We are given a huge capacity for wholeness, wonder, surprise, love, peace, joy and generosity. Each of us is gifted at birth with a tender heart, one that is filled with caring and longing and vulnerability, but is, at the same time, fragile and easily broken, one that has the capacity to expand and contract, to embrace or shut down. This heart is our basic goodness, our inherent connection to all that is sacred and pure and clean. There is no hatred, evil, bitterness, desperation or despair in our original condition.

Certainly in our beginnings there are moments of pain, hunger, reactions to wetness or cold or loud noises. There are times when the infant cries out to be held or thrashes about in its crib to get a better position. These are moments of uncontaminated pain, simple discomforts that signal need, initiate change and help reestablish equilibrium. These are purposeful pains, friendly reminders that stir the baby to act, to ask for help, to make appropriate changes. There is no extra baggage, no time when the infant reflects on his discomfort and doubts his worthiness to be alive. There are no questions about God's goodness, no feelings of hatred toward others or the environment, no negativity toward its own sense of need.

The infant has no shame in asking for help, does not remain in this state and has no need to compare its pain with that of others or to cause pain for anyone else. There is no regret over past hurt and no anxiety over the possibility of a future time when it may become hungry or wet again. We might think of this pain that is free of suffering as "good" pain, pain that helps us negotiate the land mines of human life without interfering with our basic sanity. This sort of pain is experienced directly and fully in the now and then released. There is no regretting that it happened, no self-hatred or unforgiveness attached to it. It is not indulged, enhanced, resisted or feared. It just is. This sort of pain doesn't interfere with our original innocence and basic happiness.

Then at some point our pain turns into suffering. We find ourselves wounded and, instead of moving past it, we become stuck. We can't let it go. We begin to reflect on it and assign blame, thinking it our fault, our parents' fault or God's fault. We want revenge or feel sorry for ourselves. We become angry and unhappy. We expect more negativity in the future. We have not yet learned that everything serves a purpose and that this pain is there to help move us along. Our particular pain seems different. For one reason or another we don't think we can just forget about it. We cannot forgive and we cannot move on. We are not willing to let ourselves or our enemies off the hook. We begin to look for an unrealistic cure or a way to avoid all pain. We begin to believe that we can do something to protect ourselves from ever being hurt again. We build up walls around our tender hearts. Through this process we become callous, lonely, cruel, lost and unhappy.

Dealing with Hurts

Old hurts from long ago may fester and build up an entire system of unhealthy psychological germs around it. Then smaller, insignificant jabs later open up the old wounds, reminding us of them or adding to their intensity. Over time we become less resilient and more resistant to change. We are unable to tolerate more pain or loss because we are still unstable and unsteady from previous ones. Defenses once built to shield us now trip us up and close us in.

Perhaps we cannot even identify how or where or when we were wounded. We may not be able to identify exactly which loss or disappointment really did us in, but it is there, beneath all our efforts to cover it up or forget about it. There, just beneath the surface that's tearing apart, is our initial innocence and capacity for being happily alive. It may be more than one thing. It may have occurred years ago or just yesterday. Something has wounded us so badly that we have thought about giving up. Perhaps you have had the idea that you deserve to be punished, that others will be better off without you or that your wounds will never heal.

All of this is common and all of us experience it to some degree or another. However, it does not have to be this way. We will always have pain, disappointment, loss, imperfection and failure, but we do not have to endure suffering, despair, hopelessness and self-hatred. These are not "natural"; they are not an important, integral or healthy part of living and growing. Take guilt as an example. Guilt is great for letting us know we have betrayed our own conscience, harmed our loved ones or failed in our responsibilities. Without guilt we become antisocial, corrupt and cruel. Yet excessive guilt will make us weak and ineffectual, helplessly trapped in remorse. Only a moderate dose of guilt combined with self-forgiveness and understanding can lead to improvement and healing.

Every negative feeling or thought that leads one to give up or want to commit suicide is certain to be an exaggerated and irrational version of its counterpart. Reasonable guilt becomes unbearable shame, sadness turns into oppressive despair and anger is converted into irrational rage. Humans are designed to experience anger, sadness or regret, but they are not meant to be destroyed by these experiences. We are created with vulnerabilities as well as the capacity to heal. To experience one without the other is a sure sign we have lost a portion of our humanity. This does not mean we are "crazy," deformed or stupid. It simply means we have been hurt and have temporarily been unable to figure out what to do about it.

An Alternative Diagnosis

Whatever else you may have thought about your despair, whatever names you might have given yourself, whatever labels you may have accepted from others, whatever you might have believed or denied about your condition in the past, I would like to offer this alternative "diagnosis." Think of the suicidal state of mind as a function of hurt. It may be that you also have another medical or psychiatric "diagnosis" as well, but give yourself this much respect and recognize that part of what is "wrong" with you is that you have simply been wounded.

Wounded people are not crazy. You probably have good reason to feel overwhelmed. You are not a bad person. You don't deserve to die. Dying will not fix what is broken. There is no reason to think you can't recover from this. You are worthy of being healed and helped. You have a right to be forgiven, to get back up for another round, to start over one more time. There is nothing you have done or thought or felt that has not already been experienced by others who have proven that this too can be defeated and overcome. All of this is temporary. It can and will change. You can change.

All of your raging, drinking, fighting, crying, hiding and wounding of yourself has been your way of trying to cope, of trying to escape or kick and claw your way through. This is not all bad, but it becomes destructive and ineffective whenever your negative energies are locked in and permanently targeted against your self. Self-blame and neurotic guilt only make matters worse. You have the power, the option, to let that go.

It may sound obvious or overly simplified to make such a big deal about the fact that you are first of all a hurting human being. This truth often gets lost beneath a pile of diagnostic psychobabble, technical wizardry or philosophical speculation. It is a fact that is often overlooked. In the humiliation and weakness of our darkest hour it is at times easier to think of our self as weak, sick or lacking in some way rather than to realize we are merely hurt. It can be painful to recognize our brokenness.

However, it is worse to overlook it. Ignoring our wounded condition makes it easier for us to wound ourselves further by blaming, punishing ourselves and calling ourselves names rather than working toward understanding, forgiveness and healing. It makes it easier for us to focus on the "cause" of the present wounds rather than on the condition and the cure. Forgetting that we are despondent because we have been hurt allows us to overlook the fact that wounds are temporary problems, that wounds can heal and that wounds are not helped by blame, shame or further insult.

Just as an aggressive and angry dog calls forth an aggressive response and a wounded one brings about a compassionate response, so too, when you see your self as a "bad dog," you tend to want to retaliate with punishment, cruelty, control and dominance. If we can understand ourselves as wounded pups, it may become easier for us to have some compassion toward ourselves.

The Inability to Understand Pain

Maybe you have become mired in your pain because you have failed to understand it as pain. Perhaps you have misunderstood your discouragement and thought of it as a permanent condition rather than a temporary wound. Maybe you have been approaching whatever is wrong with your life as if it were some horrible evil that requires your aggression. Maybe your aggression, anger, impatience, unforgiveness and ignorance have been adding to the pain rather than allowing it to heal.

If so, that's okay. We start from where we are. However, we must recognize what we are doing to ourselves. Our inability to understand our pain, our failure to act wisely, our lack of compassion and wisdom, our inability to keep our hearts open and to grow through these lessons are merely other aspects of our imperfect human condition. They, too, are part of our woundedness.

Do not be angry at yourself for having been angry. Do not call yourself stupid for having acted so. Right now you can begin to refuse to hate yourself for having hated yourself, to stop beating yourself up for how you have beat yourself up in the past. You can begin to heal as you reexamine your present condition and see that you are a wounded soul in need of love, care, patient attention, skilled help and time. If you don't start by giving these things to yourself, you will never heal.

When the renowned Julian of Norwich received her *Revelations of Divine Love* in the fourteenth century, she said the "vision's purpose" was to reveal that "God wants us to know that he keeps us safe both in well and in woe, and loves us as much in the hard times as the good." Moreover, she said, God wants us to know that to "succumb to pain in sorrow and mourning is not his will—rather we should quickly move on, and cling to that endless joy which is God almighty, our lover and keeper."[1]

Everyone who is given the miracle of life is also endowed with a heart that can heal. You have the innate capacity to heal, to open to the healing forces of love, grace, forgiveness and newness of life. It is the desire and plan of the divine originator of life that you find forgiveness and joy.

Just as there are automatic, natural and intelligent processes superior to anything you could ever imagine, right now, within your bloodstream, that are ready to respond immediately if you cut yourself with a razor, so there are also metaphysical "forces" within you that are prepared to assist in the healing of your spiritual, emotional and mental wounds. In just the same way that your blood cells can coagulate your blood, reduce blood loss, numb the pain and begin to close the wound after you have been physically cut, the same can occur in the realm of your psychic and emotional wounds. If these internal "forces" have not yet provided adequate healing, it is only because you have inadvertently interfered with their work by introducing other toxins such as doubt, unforgiveness, additional self-injurious thoughts or behaviors, impatience, aggression and inattentiveness.

Self-Inflicted Wounds

Perhaps you have been wounded by an unfortunate set of circumstances, maybe you have been the victim of a deliberate attack, but I am willing to bet that your greatest wounds have come from yourself. Far worse than any harm inflicted by outside forces in the past is how you presently continue to destroy yourself from within by the way you beat yourself up for your failures, how you run yourself into the ground, ridicule your weaknesses, mock your dreams, feed your bitterness and fear and ignore your own needs for respect, love and acceptance.

Imperfections, failures, losses and torments are part of human life. They do not prove that you are destined for failure, show that you are weaker than others or imply that you cannot get up. They simply mean you have fallen, and as a human, you have the right to fall. In fact, you have no other choice. You have to fall. Everyone falls and gets hurt. Everyone is called to get back up. That is the "gospel truth"; it is the truth of the gospel, the "good news" that Jesus brought to all. He said, "Indeed, God did not send the Son into the world to condemn the world, but in order that the world might be saved through him."[2] True religion is not about condemnation, but about another chance. Jesus told Peter to forgive those who offended him "not seven times, but, I tell you, seventy-seven times," which is sometimes translated as "seven times seventy." Christ wants us to offer a great many more chances for forgiveness than we would think is reasonable. This applies to our forgiveness toward others but equally applies to how relentlessly God forgives us over and over again and, indeed, must also apply to how frequently we must be willing to forgive ourselves.[3]

The unsatisfactory nature of everything we touch and are touched by is inherent in the incomprehensible plan of the universe. It does not mean God is absent or unkind. Nor does it mean that some deity is intentionally punishing us or bringing evil our way. It does not mean we are uniquely destined to remain lost or broken. It is just the way things are, and we do not always understand why. However, one thing seems certain: of all the billions of lost souls in the world, which includes everyone born into human form, some find their way back to God and heal while others remain lost and broken.

Depression, despair, hopelessness and suicidal intentions are manifestations of a lost and broken condition. These are manifestations of darkness and death rather than of wakefulness and life. More accurately, they are manifestations of our inability to adequately integrate and deal with our brokenness, that is, the inability to find forgiveness and love, the inability to accept ourselves and the world as it is. It is the absence of light and hope.

Everyone becomes broken and lost, wandering in the dark, exiled from home and unsure of what to do next. Everyone in this condition is given a measure of light, a path to follow and a hope, but we just do not always see it.

Following the Light

Not everyone follows or accepts the light and the path that is offered. The most curious thing about us when we are lost or hurt or in darkness is that we do not always want to find our way out. Although the darkness has already been dispelled by the great light of the love of God in Christ, we often refuse it. Jesus said, "…light has come into the world, and people loved darkness rather than light because their deeds were evil."[4]

So we reject the light of his love because we fear it will burn us up or scold us and make us feel inadequate and foolish. We think maybe we can hide what we are, so we move toward greater and denser forms of darkness and further into the abyss of despair, heartsickness and alienation.

The promise of salvation, in Christ's mind, was far different from some evangelical sales pitch meant to recruit people into conformity and moral perfection, to strip away their humanity or to make them into robots of pious routine and ritual. No, quite the contrary, he was promising liberation, freedom from all condemnation and self-enmity, a healing of all of our estrangements and dark places and the fulfillment of our deepest longings for love and self-realization.

The light is on our side. It contains the promise of absolute blessedness that can only be found in being loved for just exactly who and what we are. This light is the love of a father, not the judgment of some cruel king. Light brings cheer and warmth and there is nothing to fear.

It seems incredible, almost unbelievable, that anyone would want to miss out on this. Even after some of us have experienced the light and have known firsthand the dissolution of our fears and sorrows in the presence of this light, we still from time to time step off into the night again. However, we can return over and over again and, in time, if we are persistent, we will become so accustomed to the light that the darkness will begin to lose its appeal.

The Need for Healing

If the root of your despair lies somewhere in the fact that you have been hurt, then you must consider that those wounds need, deserve and require time to heal. Wounded people can heal but they need bandaging, antiseptic cream, care and patience, not aggression or indifference. Further negativity and hurt only complicate and deepen the wounds and prolong the recovery time and, at times, it can even turn a relatively minor wound into a fatal one.

Whether your wounds have been many or few, large or small, self-inflicted or caused by another makes little difference in how healing takes place. Healing is a work of grace. It begins with a willingness to allow ourselves to be healed. It demands that we respect the "territory" in which the healing is to begin. It requires that we accept ourselves just as we are, broken and wounded. It asks of us a measure of hope and faith and that we believe we can and will heal. No more difficult than having the "faith" that a cut on your finger will heal, some things we naturally trust. It is not so different with a heart wound or a rip in your very being. We simply have to learn again how to allow the healing to occur. We must clean the wounds, stitch any gaping openings, apply the salve, bandage the exposed areas and let the healing take place over time.

Later, as we improve, we become more adept at protecting ourselves from unnecessary insults and pain, to endure unavoidable pains and to learn especially how to avoid adding to ourselves the deeper wounds of self-hatred and rejection. From these beginnings we can make movement and improve, not by avoiding ever being hurt again, but by minimizing the damage every time, soothing the wounds, protecting those affected areas, treating the infection, hearing what our pain is trying to teach us and by eliminating—at all costs—our habit of turning against our self.

For now, we begin by bringing gentleness to our wounded hearts, which is a way of allowing in the first ray of light.

CHAPTER 3
Can a Suicide Be Prevented?

In the final analysis, the suicidal individual is the only one who can truly prevent his own suicide. Consider the facts. If a person is determined to kill himself, there can be no "prevention." He will not stop himself, and no one else will be able to stop him for more than a day or two. Any seriously suicidal person can quite easily foil the best prevention efforts of others. The prevention of suicide, at the most critical juncture, depends on a person's willingness to be helped or to help himself. That "willingness" may very well depend on how well he understands his options, his situation, the nature of healing and the suicidal mind.

This is not meant to suggest the suicidal person can fix herself. If we have scraped an emotional knee, we can simply slap an emotional Band-Aid on ourselves. However, if we have turned against ourselves with murderous intent or have lost all hope, we will need a more radical change in the depths of our being. Understanding and information are important, as is medication, or perhaps a change in the situation. Fundamentally, something deeper is broken and must be healed. This "something" is our existential being, the inner self, what we might call soul. Soul work is what we are talking about.

Soul Work

Soul work takes a lot of effort, but it also takes a lot of letting go; it requires knowledge as well as an awareness of the limits of knowledge, and it speaks to the depths of the individual, yet it need not be faced alone. To prepare the soul's ship for the journey back to wholeness, one must be willing to hoist the sails, set the beam and man the tiller, yet she must be equally willing to depend on the wind, to recognize her utter dependence on something other and greater than her own power. The flight from suicidal despair hinges on one's willingness to choose to set sail, yet this very choice may initially be difficult to make.

A person in despair needs and deserves help, and that help is available. However, being helped, receiving help or even being put into a position to be able to help oneself first requires that one be "willing." Willingness involves a choice, a willingness to lay oneself bare, to no longer hide and to speak of one's despair to others. It is not entirely dependent on individual will. More complicated still is the fact that we may not even be able to find ourselves willing to be without grace first drawing us forth.

In any event, we must be willing "to be willing." We must invite healing to happen. We must believe it is possible. Jesus consistently taught that people would get about as much happiness, holiness, healing or love as they were willing to believe in and receive. He never pushed these graces on anyone, but he never withheld them from those of sincerity and faith. Those who knock with the intent of getting in will find that the door opens. Jesus was saying something very important about people getting what they most desire. For the suicidal person, this is a promise of abundant life to anyone who wants to live.

This is not as easy as it sounds because it is not always easy to want to live. We do not always ask for and believe in what is best for us. Many of the things we want for ourselves or say we want are actually things we do not want. Other things that we honestly want, like a serious romantic relationship, are things we often unconsciously sabotage. This explains why diets, New Year's resolutions and cigarette smoking cessation programs so frequently fail. An active alcoholic finds it nearly impossible to truly "ask for" and "believe in" sobriety because what one really wants is to continue drinking. Susan Rose Blauner, a woman who was chronically suicidal for many years, admitted that she was "addicted" to suicidal thinking, and she said that "Letting go of suicide was the hardest thing I've ever had to do."[1]

To "believe" life is unlivable is to make it so. However, to believe that life is a wonder and a surprise is also a way to activate the power of life's wonder and surprise, and then to see this power manifest in daily life.

Sick people who give up the will to live, who really prefer to die, die much quicker than others with the same illness who really want to live. We know that elderly persons may die soon after their spouses' deaths because they have lost their reason to want to live.

The "will to live" is one of the most important and powerful determinants in the outcome of many life-threatening illnesses, and many surgeons will refuse to operate on someone who believes they will die on the operating table. This is even more true for those illnesses that are essentially psychological or spiritual from the start, such as many cases involving despair or suicidal thinking. Suicidal despair could in fact be defined as an absence of, or weakness in, the will to live. When the will to live is recovered or strengthened, suicidal thinking disappears. We know that most people who are discouraged, sad and beaten down by life, more often than not get back up. This occurs due to the fact that these people, on the deepest levels, want to get up.

If we are to find our way back up we must rediscover the will to live. It is not required that we "feel" like living at first, or that we completely believe in living or that we even know exactly what it will take to make our life fully livable again, but initially, in the beginning, it takes a *willingness* to be *willing* to get up and try again.

The Will to Live

This willingness to live is not the same as "will power," or willfulness. In many ways it is the opposite. A willingness to allow life to do its thing, to trust it to carry us through, a willingness to be wrong and to depend on life is to prove it is right. According to psychologist Gerald May, we have essentially three choices. "Willingness and willfulness become possibilities every time we truly engage life. There is only one other option—to avoid the engagement entirely."[2] To avoid the engagement entirely is to be suicidal, and to be willful in our will power alone is to set ourselves up for the same kind of fall that made us suicidal in the first place.

May recommends the third option: *to be willing*. He further clarifies by saying that "willingness implies a surrendering of one's self-separateness, an entering-into, an immersion in the deepest processes of life itself. It is a realization that one already is a part of some cosmic process and it is a commitment to participate in that process. In contrast, willfulness is the setting of oneself apart from the fundamental essence of life in an attempt to master, control, or otherwise manipulate existence."[3]

In the battle for a renewed will to live we must surrender the illusion of being in control of life or even of our own will. Does this sound unusual? It may, but it is central to our turning back into life, for we have already discovered the impossibility of making life conform to our will, and we have flirted with avoiding the fight altogether. Now, we are being challenged to take a new and radical approach: *Let go. Trust. Be.* This is the part that we "do." The rest must come from beyond our individual selves.

We all need other people, outside assistance and something more than what we can generate on our own power from time to time. We are dependent on forces larger than ourselves, if nothing more than air and gravity, food and water, the automatic beating of our hearts. The will to live is a willingness to accept this dependency, to trust rather than to continue fighting and forcing things. The will to live is open, vulnerable, accepting, and as we explore this understanding further we will appreciate how this can help us heal.

This learning "how to be willing" and "how to let go into life" may be compared to how one learns to ride a bicycle. The willingness to ride a bike is not the same as the "ability" to ride correctly but is rather the initial willingness to get up and try over and again until it is accomplished. The will to live is the deep intent to survive along with the still deeper conviction that life survives and that we are a small particle of that which survives all manner of disappointment, loss and pain.

This is difficult to ask of a person in despair. By definition, the suicidal person does not necessarily want to be willing. They may not believe help is possible or that they deserve it. The first thing to understand about the suicidal condition is just this: any reluctance one may feel about getting help, whatever negativity they have about the real possibility of wellness and all those feelings of unworthiness and doubt are manifestations of the sickness that has temporarily attached to them. It is not the "real" soul of the person as much as it is a manifestation of an illness. The fact that an individual has considered killing oneself, that he faces doubts about living at all indicates that the "illness" has deteriorated his best and truest self and has negatively altered his best judgment and wisest perception. This "illness" is foreign to who he was meant to be and has progressed to the point that he needs some help to see past it. If you have been one of these people but are now reading this for yourself, it is an indication that you have already taken an initial step toward this process. It is proof that you still have the capacity, the ability, to exert your willingness to get to the place you deserve to be.

To suggest that a suicidal person can understand and prevent her own suicide may be a bit like telling someone with a toothache that she doesn't have to suffer with the pain any longer. She may argue that there is nothing she can do and that over-the-counter pain medicines don't offer relief, that biting down doesn't help, that leaving it alone doesn't help, that pulling it out doesn't seem possible and that there is nothing she can do to stop the pain. We may understand and agree with how that person feels, but we would also immediately assert that there is something she can do. She can go to a dentist. If she insisted that all dentists are quacks or that she cannot afford that kind of help, we would stand firm in our knowledge that help is not only possible but that the right kind of help could certainly offer a huge relief. Regardless of what we might say or believe about the situation, if the person with the toothache refused to make a move, we would then be forced to concede the point, knowing the situation will not improve without her cooperation even though it easily could with it.

Suicidal Despair

This is how it is with recovering from suicidal despair. One must be willing to take another chance on life. So the next step in helping yourself or someone else to prevent a suicide is to recognize this despair. We must remind them or ourselves that there are options; things can improve and things will certainly change if we hang in there long enough. One of the great mysteries of God's grace is that it is still actively at work in us even when it appears to be absent. We might not always be able to "help ourselves" in the sense of diagnosing the problem or completing all of the actual work that may be required, but we can get ourselves to someone who knows what to do—like God, a psychiatrist or your own true original self—preferably all three.

Some suicidal people may not like doctors or trust others or God. They may no longer believe in themselves, that they are worthy of being helped or that they can be helped. None of these things need stop them from reaching out. In order to set sail, it is not required that we understand everything about wind or that we have absolute trust in the wind after having witnessed all the terrible things it can do. We just have to remember that the wind is also full of good and useful power if we are willing to align ourselves to it with proper preparations and patience. It takes courage and faith to pull up the sails again after we have been shipwrecked or left stranded on the seas so many times before. Yet there is no other way to leave the shore of our despair without some trust and risk taking. Without this willingness to risk another chance, the despairing individual will be lost forever. All we need to begin is the willingness to begin. Grace will pick up where our resources leave off.

There will be many obstacles and disappointments. We may have already tried to set sail but have once again failed, been mistreated or have tried medication, psychotherapy or hospitals with little success. We might have a small old boat with few accessories. We may doubt ourselves and others, but we can try again. None of these obstacles can keep our sailing vessel from gaining momentum and moving off into a new direction toward another shore. Refusing to pull up the sails or imagine ourselves sailing into a better world will shut us down for as long as we refuse. We have that choice, that decision to make. No one else can make it for us.

We have the freedom and the responsibility to try again until it works. The despairing person can easily become a hopeful person full of the promises and surprises that make life an adventure again with just the smallest gust of wind, the least little turn of fortune. I have seen suicidal crack-addicted prostitutes restored to sanity in less than six months, but I have never seen it happen to one who refuses treatment or to at least cooperate with forced treatment once it is put in motion. This is the willingness to pull up the sails. That may be all we can muster at first, and that, along with a little breeze, is enough to get going. Apart from that we stay put. We do not control the breeze, but we are in charge of the sails.

The first thing the suicidal person needs to do is to stay in the boat and keep it afloat. Don't jump overboard or drill a hole in the bottom. Even if you have only the smallest dying glimmer of hope left, as long as you stay afloat you have a fighting chance. That simple yet profound movement is enough to plant a seed for the future. When that beautiful southerly breeze begins to lift and the sun appears on the horizon, you will be right where you need to be in order to ride out of that port you have been trapped in all these months or years.

The smallest speck of belief, combined with a willingness to let it grow, is like the "mustard seed" of faith mentioned in the New Testament. You do not need a ton of it. Everyone has already been given a measure of it. You only need to take the tiniest bit and protect it, water it and give it time. It will grow into a great tree, and in that tree you will find shade and partake of its many fruits. The smallest willingness to get through your suicidal crises is already there, and that is the seed of your future salvation.

Although despair or suicidal thinking is most likely interrelated to some other condition that may require medical attention, such as mental illness, addiction or an incurable illness, the first concern is not medical, but spiritual: this willingness to try again, to believe again just once more and to seek and accept help. Without that initial spark, the underlying or contributing illness will never receive proper treatment.

Every suicidal person can be helped, and every suicide can be prevented *"IF...."* Not if you're lucky, not if you're rich, not if you are smart or saintly or strong enough, but simply because you are courageous enough to make that first critical move. You can prevent yourself from going through with suicide and begin the healing journey, any time you are ready.

Accepting Help

The next most important thing to understand, after understanding the fact that we *can* be helped and that it is up to us to allow ourselves to be helped, is to recognize the fact that we cannot do it alone. Perhaps a person can move off from shore through an artificial power, such as a small outboard motor, but the problem is that the motor will run out of gas or burn itself out. Setting out on our own power alone is never enough; we will ultimately need others, and God as well, if we are to travel very far.

The other problem we encounter in the suicidal situation is that the one most likely to captain the boat from the harbor is also the one most likely to capsize the boat. Suicidal people shoot themselves in the foot, literally and figuratively. They are already partially against themselves by nature of their suicidal thoughts and self-destructive impulses. This takes some time to change. In the initial months of recovery such a person may need a sailing instructor, a cocaptain, some information and encouragement or a good first mate.

In a paradoxical vein, the suicidal person can truly prevent her own self-imposed death by first taking a willing step of faith. Yet again, I suggest such a person may not be able to do it alone. This is where the "willingness" to get well so often includes the willingness to be helped by others. When one is feeling suicidal, when suicide appears to be a logical or sane solution, when thoughts of death continually reoccur and the wish, intent or plan for suicidal activity is observed, that is the time to recognize that you need additional help. The enemy is now inside; your own worst enemy has emerged from within, and you cannot always get rid of this part of yourself without a little help. Similar to the previous example of a person needing a dentist, it would be cruel and unfair to expect the suicidal person to do one's own root canal.

It is not normal, healthy, reasonable or realistic to think suicide is the solution to our problems. To have those thoughts is the first sign that we have become deluded, confused or misled by the illness, trauma or disappointment we are currently experiencing. The suicidal individual can prevent this disordered thinking from becoming a completed act of suicide.

Suicidal feelings or thoughts are a by-product of another "illness," and whether that illness happens to be called clinical depression, fatal anger, chronic pain, irrational or delusional thinking, drug or alcohol abuse or dependence, post–traumatic stress disorder, some medical condition, uncontrollable anxiety, spiritual crisis or one of various other similar disorders, these conditions require professional attention. For example, if you just discovered that you have a brain tumor, you do not have the time or luxury to sit around and worry about it, blame yourself that it is there or hope that it will go away on its own. You need help, and even if that brain tumor begins to cloud your judgment a bit, even if some part of you says no to accepting help, you must get help or allow yourself to be helped anyway, trusting the judgment of professional opinion and those around you who have your best interest at heart.

Suicidal thinking is not a sign of inadequacy, moral weakness or some personal flaw. It is an illness that requires and responds to treatment. The majority of those who go through a suicidal crisis and are helped later look back on it and thank their lucky stars they did not kill themselves while in a temporary state of shock, confusion, rage or sadness. The majority of persons considering suicide are candidates for antidepressant, antianxiety or antipsychotic medication. They are frequently in need of detoxification from drugs or alcohol. They may need financial assistance, like food stamps or subsidized shelter. Others are battling chronic pain or some major illness, both of which clearly need medical attention. There are uncontrollable and unforeseen circumstances, unmanageable predicaments and complex forces at work undermining your sanity and making suicide seem like a reasonable idea. None of these things can be handled alone, nor should they be.

No one wants to suffer. Nobody plans to become suicidal. Suicidal thinking comes into play after other solutions or options have been considered or tried and when one loses the ability to see hope or a reason to live. Sometimes it is an impulsive, unthinking or explosive reaction. Nobody plans that either. If suicidal people could simply prevent their own crises, conditions or situations without getting a little outside help, they would not become suicidal.

They must know they are making the decisions. They are not in control of all the bad feelings, the depression, the addiction, poverty, loss and grief they are experiencing. They may not be able to control any of that right now on their own, but they can control whether they will try to kill themselves or not.

Suicide Is a Choice

In fact, control is often the appeal of suicide, what draws the individual into the downward spiral. It is the only thing a person "completely out of control" can still control. The fates may seem to be out of control, our life may appear to be out of control, our loved ones may have died or left or betrayed us beyond our control, cancer may have taken us into the bowels of hell apart from our choice or control, but taking our own life may seem to be the one thing left that we can control.

Suicide, then, can even appear to be a means of gaining back some control of fate, others, ourselves or the world around us. It may at times seem as if killing ourselves might force some change in fate, others, destiny or the world at large. Like the Buddhist monk who set himself on fire in protest of the Vietnam War, we sometimes feel as if our suicide might once and for all make things right, but this is an illusion. There are still wars. People will continue to disappoint, there will always be inequality and unfairness, people will go on dying and lying and cheating, and the world will go right on as it was before our death with the additional sorrow and negative example we have left behind.

Many times when people are feeling suicidal, they report the feeling or suspicion that they may not be able to control their suicidal impulses. Some report feeling as if they are driven to it. Seriously ill patients sometimes hear voices that command them or tell them to do it. Anxious and obsessive types become afraid that they might "snap" and do it even when they don't want to.

The truth of the matter is that we are always in control of this decision. The power over whether or not we will try to kill ourselves is left to us. No one can make us do it. Your "nerves," bad feelings, powerful negative thoughts or persistent pain cannot force you to kill yourself. Even expert exorcists who deal in cases of actual demonic possession tell us that the devil himself must obtain the consent of a person's will before he can exert any actual control over a life, and that, even then, one retains control of his own will.

When it comes to suicide as a potential outcome of my life, as the final destiny in my ongoing drama, it is I alone who writes the script. I determine my own fate, at least in regard to this one decision. "Determining my own fate" sounds a bit lofty.

It is not that we can control or decide much of anything else. The future continues on without our consent, and the past cannot be changed. We can, however, decide whether or not to kill ourselves. If a person cannot make a rational decision about this because of mental illness, brain atrophy, retardation or any other reason, someone else will have to make that decision for them. If someone you care about lacks this capacity and is suicidal, I suggest you contact local police or suicide prevention experts to intervene. For the typical despairing individual who is contemplating suicide, there is help and hope, as long as they admit to their condition and allow others to reach them.

Putting Grace in Motion

Every time we make the decision to live, to ask for help, to forgo the option to kill ourselves, we are opening the doors to our future. We are putting in motion a whole host of possibilities and potentialities that lie within us and in God, our community and a whole network of professional helpers, loved ones and perhaps even saints and angels. Help of this sort is what might be considered to be "motions of grace." We might begin with a wonderful quote from Nicholas of Cusa, a noted theologian from the 1400s: "Lord, Thou has given me my being of such a nature that it can continually make itself more able to receive thy grace and goodness. And this power…is free will. By this I can either enlarge or restrict my capacity for thy grace."[4]

Choosing to live can at times be the most courageous thing a person can do. To be willing to learn how to love life can be the first step toward a great awakening. The capacity to love life as it is, regardless of what it brings, is one of the distinguishing marks of complete mental wellness and characterizes the saints and spiritual masters of all times. Emotionally and spiritually healthy people are no more exempt from the disabling and contradictory ugliness of life than we are. It is just that they have understood how to love life completely as it is.

In this loving embrace, life is transformed from something to be feared into something to be celebrated. The very act of being grateful for life, of seeking more of life and engaging in its mischief wholeheartedly is what changes one's life in the world. The lover of life is no longer afraid of its uncertainties, anxious about tomorrow's problems or engaged in the desperate attempt to forget the past or avoid the present. Such individuals have learned to be content with things as they are, and they trust that all things are as they should be. By loving life, we become more aware of its lovable aspects and respond more readily to its embrace.

Conversely, those of us who reject life, who resist its ways and are in constant opposition to what is, while chasing down what could or should be, are destined to remain unsettled and at odds with themselves and the world. There is no place to rest for the person who resists life as it is. "The surest test if a man be sane," writes the Taoist sage Lao Tzu, is if he "accepts life whole, as it is." This is not only the sure sign of sanity, but the beginning of a truly realized life.[5]

In a fictionalized account of the life of St. Francis, Christian Bobin describes a critical turning point in the life of this simple monk who was to become one of the most beloved of all saints. Francis says, "Today I have found something greater than my dream. Love has awakened my sleeping life. I have found life. I am leaving to go to that life. I will do battle for that life, and I will serve its name. Life comes to me from life, and it is toward that that I am going, toward my lover with the eyes of snow, my little wellspring, my only wife. Life. Nothing but life. Life, all of life."[6]

This awakening and commitment to all of life changed the quality and course of Francis's existence. He was no longer double minded, uncertain and misled. He took upon himself the identity of a keeper of life, a lover of all life. He accepted as his calling and mission in life to support and protect and celebrate life on every occasion and in all its manifestations. He took life upon himself as if it were his lover and spouse, as if God and all living creatures were one and the same. In choosing life, he embraced times of happiness and trouble, and in doing so he broke through to a joy beyond natural pleasures or a simple adjustment to living, becoming full of the joy of God himself.

Our free will, the responsibility and privilege of choosing what we will do about our illness remains within our range of possible options. Unless we are brain damaged or mentally incompetent, we are blessed, and in some sense cursed, with the responsibility of directing our will either toward or away from death as well as toward or away from grace.

William James once wrote, "Be not afraid of life. Believe that life is worth living, and your belief will help create the fact."[7] This is not merely one man's philosophy but a metaphysical fact.

CHAPTER 4
Understanding the Suicidal Condition

Hemingway once observed, "Life breaks us all," but that some "become strong at the broken places."[1] He proved this true by converting his own brokenness, heartache and longing into some of the most outstanding literature ever produced by an American writer. He became strong at his broken places. Then he shot himself in the head.

There has been much made of his "depression" and "paranoia," his alcohol abuse, tumultuous relationships, macho persona, artistic temperament, failing health and familiarity with guns, all of which contributed to his demise, but in the end, what do you think killed Hemingway?

His son, Gregory, gives us an intimate peek into his condition. Toward the end, Greg notes, his dad had lost much of his creative powers. The "world no longer flowed through him as through a purifying filter, with the distillate seeming more true and beautiful than the world itself." He was "no longer a poet" and had witnessed the demise of his own genius. He was faced with the "knowledge of what it was like for the rest of the people all of the time to be uncushioned from the world by the intellectual and material rewards of genius." He was forced to deal with his humanity, weakness, vulnerability and, most of all, the loss of that creative core he had come to understand as the core of his very being. This condition Gregory accurately referred to as "dry rot of the soul."[2]

The soul in Hemingway began to rot. He watched as his artistic and creative powers withered, and he could do nothing to stop it. There was torment and heartbreak in those months as his ego identity gave way to the mental weakness, fatigue and lack of control that will sooner or later get us all. It was not the booze or illness or misfortune that pulled the trigger. It was Ernest, our beloved Papa himself, who could not face another day with such sickness of soul.

Years before, his periods of brokenness and heartsickness were made strong through strength of soul, through the hope of his vision, the love of his gift and his faith in art. He could "filter and distill" life and make it more beautiful than it actually was. But when that failed, he snapped apart at the broken places.

Hemingway could not tolerate the loss of his imagination and the gift that he had come to understand as his true and only life. A short time before his suicide, he confided in his longtime friend A. E. Hotchner, "Hotch, if I can't exist on my own terms, then existence is impossible." Hotchner observed that as a younger man Hemingway had never been feeble artistically, intellectually or physically, "and when he became so he refused to accept it."[3]

Son Gregory also saw something else in him months before he died: "…it was as if he had already given up."[4] Another friend said, "It will take some time to wear him out. And before that he will be dead."[5] His own psychiatrist theorized that his symptoms were "related to his impoverishment as a writer, with attendant jeopardy to his identity and stature."[6] Hemingway himself, as well as those close to him, seemed to recognize it was this "soul rot," "identity loss," "giving up" and "refusal to accept" existence on its own terms that made living impossible for him at this stage. Gregory adds, "He never could develop a philosophy of life that would allow him to grow old gracefully."[7]

The Importance of One's View of the World

Now Hemingway is only one man, but his story is quite instructive. Self-destructive, hopeless and suicidal individuals typically face a similar onslaught of physical, mental or emotional illness. The difference between those who survive and those who destroy themselves lies in the soul. One's worldview and self have as much to do with the impact of suffering as does the nature and extent of the suffering itself. One's life philosophy will determine whether one can accept life on its own terms and adjust to it as it presents itself or be crushed by its seemingly cruel indifference. A person's capacity to hope and have faith in troubled times differentiates the winner from the loser. The willingness to relinquish control and leave ego behind when there seems to be little other choice is what separates the saintly from the insane. The presence or absence of love is often the thing that breaks the camel's back. All of these and more are qualities of the soul. Suicide is, to borrow Greg's term, a product of "soul rot," and survivorship is dependent on the health of the soul.

One can potentially defeat self-destructive urges and despair through soul vitality. By fortifying, refreshing and nourishing one's inner wealth of vision, creativity, true identity, love and transcendent hope, that is, by fortifying and purifying one's soul, one can maintain or recover the capacity to survive and thrive, to live and be alive. Just as one is dead inside long before she pulls the trigger, so the one who goes into a crisis and comes forth victorious has nourished her soul ahead of time. If the soul has been neglected, however, there is still time for a crash course in the midst of the fight.

Healing the soul is always possible, though at times it can require hard work. Not hard as in backbreaking labor or strenuous intellectual debate, but hard as in humbling one's self, surrendering one's will to God and accepting God's absolute sovereignty in all things. Even though it is a generous and wonderful gift that brings the soul to life, it can be very devastating for the person who has fancied himself independently capable and self-assured prior to the onslaught of a crisis that brings him to his knees. Anyone who has come to the point of suicidal despair has been brought to the realization of his limited power and control, and as difficult as that realization may be, it is a prerequisite for soul retrieval.

The soul can be rotten, crippled, partially weakened or, in the worst of times, dead. As one mystic put it, "The soul is dead when it never thinks of God, when it has lost all memory of God."[8] Meister Eckhart described it: "You will have peace to the extent that you have God, and the further you are away from God the less you will be at peace."[9]

It is easy to allow our souls to become neglected, rotted or diminished by pain. Everyone has the potential to undermine, defeat or even destroy their own soul. It has been suggested that earthly life is nothing less than a battleground for the soul. Jesus asks us to think about what it might mean to "gain the whole world, but lose your soul," and he warned that we should not be concerned about those people or events that can merely harm the body, but should pay close attention to him who has control over both the body and the soul. Soul recovery is everything. Soul may in fact be the same thing as what Jesus referred to as the kingdom of God, that which is now come upon you and is within you but that is so easy to miss. When we recover our soul we rediscover our truest deepest authentic self, which is one with the Self of all that is.

Instead of defending, defining and discovering soul, we spend so much of our energies working against it. Rather than thinking about God, we think only about ourselves. Instead of spending ourselves in the service of others, we pour our last dime into pleasures and vain entertainments. It is in our nature to struggle against soul while we are, at the same time, struggling to find it. We are confused as to what constitutes our true life, what really matters and what, when all is said and done, satisfies our core self. We are all caught in this basic and unavoidable dilemma from birth onward.

Whenever we reject ourselves, despise our weaknesses, criticize our looks, abuse our bodies, alienate our loved ones, spoil our potential, ridicule our dreams and undermine our own happiness, we are limiting and thwarting our soul's potential. By ignoring and forgetting God we suffocate the soul. Hating and judging others only harms our own soul. The surest sign that we are losing the battle for soul is the presence of despair, self-destructiveness, unrest, troubled relationships and unremitting sorrow.

Hemingway was certainly right about the possibility of becoming strong at the broken places. However, he did not seem to have a great deal of faith, and when his manly abilities to rebuild his life were spent, he cursed himself and died a sad death.

Soul in the Age of Science

Many recent writers have expressed concern over this generation's overly enthusiastic acceptance of the medical models' position on psychiatric disorders, especially depression and anxiety.[10] Forgoing soul and paying one-sided attention to the discovery of the role of neurotransmitters and the efficacy of medications in the treatment of mental disorders, many of us have inadvertently and subliminally been trained to assume the majority of our most severe emotions are merely "symptoms" of "disorders" that can be treated and removed through application of the correct scientific procedures. It is common for clients to consult a psychiatrist or therapist with the intent of ridding themselves of all "bad" or unwanted feelings.

Any honest and insightful person knows better. Yet we have all been enchanted to some degree, hoping that there could be, or may be, a magical pill or a simple answer for our problems. Through advertising, pressures from insurance providers and our own desire to find an easy solution, the believability of a quick fix is all too readily accepted. However, "symptoms" are very rarely indicative of disordered brain chemistry alone.

It is natural to have periods of sadness and confusion. If the drug companies ever found a way to rid ourselves of all our unacceptable feelings, we would be deprived of our humanity and our potential for the growth of our soul. "If we persist in our modern way of treating depression as an illness to be cured only mechanically and chemically, we may lose the gifts of soul that only depression can provide," writes Thomas Moore.[11] It is not only okay to be scared and sad, but it is essential. Negative emotions are often "gifts of soul" and inform us of the condition of our souls. Just as injecting your hand with pain medication would put you in danger of cutting your fingers off without even realizing it, if we were to be rid of all our disagreeable emotions we would never know when we have lost touch with God and ourselves. It is important to listen to our discomfort and to trace these feelings back to their dynamic origins.

Outside of a few rare situations involving medical disease, we can almost always assume there is a good reason for our sadness, confusion and fear. Our feelings are not mysterious, random or unreasonable. They have a meaning and a purpose. Even when brain chemistry and genetics are a factor, we can almost always identify an emotional, psychological or spiritual basis for our despair as well.

There is no clear and consistent pattern. If we accept that suicide is the result of mental, physical or social conditions, we will find that the theories do not always explain the apparently random appearance of hope and the will to fight. Some people become physically paralyzed, like Joni Erickson and Christopher Reeves, and turn their tragedies into triumphs, while others in perfect health kill themselves. Some endure the terrors of a concentration camp, like Viktor Frankl, Primo Levi or Anne Frank, only to write about it, encouraging millions of others to find hope and meaning through suffering. Yet, every day comfortable suburban teens commit suicide. Beethoven made music in his deafness, Helen Keller spoke of what she saw from her blind and mute condition. Meanwhile, a man in his early twenties with a promising future in professional baseball hangs himself for failing a course in college.

There are many complicated and competing theories regarding suicide. On one level certain "personality traits" such as heartiness, optimism, endurance and pain tolerance seem to make a difference in whether one becomes suicidal or not. We understand that social conditioning, chemical dependency, learning, age, race, family modeling and socioeconomic dynamics play a role in the prevalence of suicide. Mental illness is implicated and genetic disposition is suspected. Theories about childhood trauma, brain chemistry and past life influences abound, but none of these systems of thought seems to give much attention to the role of faith, love and hope, concepts related to the health and well-being of one's soul.

Soul Vitality

Childhood molestation is a good example of something one might imagine to be consistently related to a despairing or suicidal condition, but it is not necessarily the case. Some unidentified internal power of optimism is present in some, yet not in others.

This power to survive, fight back and overcome arises independent of other factors. Some transform these terrible experiences into a reason to never let anyone ever again trample the innocent.

Oprah Winfrey and Maya Angelou are examples of those who have turned their childhood traumas into poetry. Whatever distinguishes Maya and Oprah from those who never recover from such experiences may be due in part to social learning and genetics, but there is more afoot. It is not just a few famous exemplary women who are the only exceptions. Becoming more hearty and determined through such experiences is just as common as becoming defeated and helpless. This special something is representative of what may be called soul vitality.

Of all the things that actually lead people to suicide, we know it is not simply the nature or extent of the precipitating trauma or event. It has more to do with the internal and subjective state of the person. The only thing we know for certain is that persons who kill themselves typically suffer from feelings of helplessness, hopelessness and an unbearable subjective sense of physical or mental pain. At some point they give up. These "experiences" of hopelessness and helplessness and giving up are not related to how helpless or hopeless the person or situation actually is. Giving up is a function of soul.

It is vitality of soul that allows one to bear the unbearable, believe the unbelievable and hope for that which is not yet evident. The invincible soul triumphs over all manner of pain and evil. It is our soul that keeps us alive and allows us to overcome when all else fails.

Suicide, of course, is a term traditionally referring to self-inflicted death. But in light of soul as the keeper and defender of all manifestations of life, including physical, emotional, relational, mental and spiritual life, we can also include all movement against life in any form as a type of suicide. In other words, soul refers to all that supports, nourishes and advances life and wholeness, while suicide can refer to any behavior, thought or activity that undermines, divides, threatens or destroys it.

Following this thought, we can speculate that the life force is encouraged and enhanced by persons with a healthy soul, and that the death instinct has free rein in those with a weak or disabled soul. To say that soul encourages life-supporting activities is to say soul supports wholeness and well-being.

The meaning of well-being in this context will not necessarily correspond to popular versions of psychological, physical, spiritual or emotional "well-being" however, for soul defines wellness differently. As a brief example, popular thought assumes one should be young, healthy, beautiful and happy at all times, and that one should focus all of her efforts at obtaining and maintaining these ideals at all costs. In soul logic "well-being" includes the gracious acceptance of age, the acknowledgment of sadness as an important passage and death as the acceptable end of all living things.

In light of soul, we can begin to understand the suicidal phenomena from this broader perspective. By appreciating the role of soul as the primary force that encourages, enhances and inspires all impulses toward life in every conceivable form and by understanding the subtleties of how self-neglect, self-harm and self-sabotage are soul-sick activities, we can begin to appreciate the problem of suicide as something much broader than merely the killing of one's physical body.

Self-Destructiveness in Many Forms

All self-destructive movements are related to one another. Physical suicide is merely the most alarming manifestation of a more chronic and insidious case of self-defeat born of soul sickness.

Noted theorist Erich Fromm observed that self-destructiveness appears in proportion to the frustration of the need to fulfill one's "productive potentiality," which he characterized as the potential to love and be loved. He writes, "If life's tendency to grow, to be loved, is thwarted, the energy thus blocked undergoes a process of change and is transformed into life-destructive energy. Destructiveness is the outcome of unlived life. Those individual and social conditions that make for the blocking of life-furthering energy produce destructiveness which is in turn the source from which the various manifestations of evil spring."[12]

When the soul's thirst for life is thwarted, self-destructiveness arises. Bodily suicide is but one of the manifestations of this self-defeating and destructive impulse. Other manifestations include all manner of social, intellectual, emotional or spiritual "suicide." All levels and types of self-destructive movement can thus be considered a result of a sickened and thwarted soul.

Some of these self-destructive thoughts and behaviors are consciously chosen, but many of them are unconscious. For example, many of us habitually put ourselves down. We may automatically blame ourselves for things that go wrong and routinely withhold good feelings and pleasures from ourselves in a stance of false humility or neurotic masochistic role playing. This sort of inverted self-love is self-abuse and is a manifestation of neither wisdom nor love. It is driven by self-hatred and guilt rather than selflessness and healthy self-care. We cannot love others or God without first loving ourselves. Many such patterns of self-blame and punishments are subtle manifestations of the lack of a grace-filled soul.

Self-hatred, self-harm and self-neglect in every form, bodily or emotional, subtle or outright, reflects a lack of self-love. Self-love is the hallmark of a healthy soul. Such soul sickness is never cured by aggression or further self-rejection. Anger, punishment, negativity, worry and fear never inspire healing in the sickened soul.

St. John of Kanty advised that we should "Fight all error, but do it with good humor, patience, kindness, and love. Harshness will damage your own soul and spoil the best cause."[13] Perhaps this is precisely how we go from bad to worse when we are down. We experience failures and weaknesses, but instead of having the strength of soul to deal with ourselves graciously, we cause even greater damage to our already fractured selves by reacting harshly. We inflict injury to our health, our relationships, our spiritual life, our peace of mind and our opportunities every time we act impatiently, critically or cruelly toward our self.

It is no stretch of the imagination to consider risk-taking behaviors, addictions, excesses, toxic relationships and self-neglect as forms of self-destructiveness. All such self-destruction and aggression toward the self are signs of an unhealthy and hurting soul. When we are hurt we react with anger and fear. This anger is turned inward, and this fear becomes a fear of life, and is manifested by depression, despair and suicidal tendencies.

The ways in which we inflict pain on ourselves are endless. We deny ourselves the chance to feel good by making poor choices regarding how we behave, whom we date and where we spend our time. We abuse our bodies with toxic substances, work jobs we hate, refuse to give forgiveness to ourselves and others, make unrealistic demands on ourselves and the world, avoid God and seek out ruin at every turn. This tendency is true for the saint as well as the sinner, and even Paul the Apostle cries out, "Wretched man that I am! Who will rescue me from this body of death?" The answer, he says, is "God through Jesus Christ our Lord!"[14] He points to a spiritual cure because he knows this is a spiritual ailment. There is no stopping our self-defeating tendencies apart from grace.

No Place for Asceticism

Grace is freely given. There is no value in tormenting or disciplining the physical body, mind or soul in an effort to obtain spiritual favor. There will be plenty of crosses to bear, things we will lose and things we will long for that we will never obtain, and this alone is enough to work in us the perfect work of grace through patience and faith.[15] The real geniuses of the spiritual life, most notably Jesus and Buddha, pointed out the worthlessness of self-inflicted pain as a means of advancing the soul. They suggested self-forgiveness, moderation and fullness of joy in walking the path of love as alternatives to the self-torture, endless penances and strict methods of discipline prevalent in some sects of their day.

Jesus and Buddha never backed down from legitimate suffering, but they never encouraged it or sought it out as a means of self-improvement. When we are free and full and whole through love, grace, self-acceptance and trust, we become free to be happily alive by facing things squarely as they are. This is the tremendous thing about true faith: it offers no easy solution for evil or a quick remedy for suffering, yet just the same it allows one to bore through the impossibilities as if tunneling through an immovable rock. It offers a way of being when being seems unbearable.

Writer and Presbyterian minister Fredrick Buechner described it in the following way: "...faith is a stranger, an exile on earth, and doesn't know for certain about anything. Faith is homesickness. Faith is a lump in the throat. Faith is less a position *on* than a movement *toward*—less a sure thing than a hunch. Faith is waiting. Faith is journeying through time and space."[16] The key here is that this faith allows one to journey *through*, even when it is uncertain.

Selflessness, self-denial in compassionate actions and the wise practice of self-renunciation are all very different things from self-hatred or self-abuse. The difference between unhealthy self-hatred and rejection and a healthy self-forgetting and self-transcendence lies in the way we love our selves. True love for one's self allows the individual to leave one's own interests and attachments behind in favor of a greater good, while a neurotic attachment to the illusion of an independent self often leads one to try and harm the self in an effort to correct or undo wrongs done.

This is paradoxical but it is critical. The person lacking self-love torments, attacks, rejects and ridicules the self in an effort to rid it of faults through punishment. This reinforces the struggle of the ego and sets up a war zone within the structure of the self. No one wins. The one who loves the self wisely understands that when it is understood, accepted and forgiven, it loses its self-destructive power and need for supremacy or critical control. The loved self is free to love in return and thus, in love, to become selfless and whole. Love wins, and the self naturally assumes less and less importance. The soul is awakened and expanded through self-acceptance, self-love and self-understanding.

If we will tend to the soul's needs as manifested in the relational, personal and transcendent concerns of everyday life as they arise, we may find there will be little room for the insidious disease of self-hatred and hopelessness to continue. We can learn to replace self-defeating patterns and punishment with self-understanding and care. Rather than trying to repress our bad feelings with aggression, we can learn to accept them with gentleness. Instead of remaining fixated on a path of self-harm, we can discover ways to nurture and share our selves with others, which will in turn produce in us greater levels of meaning, purpose and fulfillment.

Tending these concerns moment to moment is what we now must learn to do. Doing so is soul work. It's life work. It must become the backbone of any darkness-dispelling and anti-suicidal strategy.

CHAPTER 5
The Promise of Soul

Maybe we give up because life is too hard? Martyrs, heroes and ordinary people who overcome adversity of every type would disagree. Life is difficult when one is at war, a quadriplegic, rejected by a lover, addicted to a drug, soiled by evil deeds or unable to accomplish all one sets out to do. However, this has not stopped millions of such afflicted individuals from surviving, rising again, finding new love, healing, recovering and rediscovering a new life.

Perhaps we give in because we have bad genes, failed parenting, a weak constitution or faulty brain chemistry. All these aspects may play a part, but there is something else, something more fundamental at work. Something deeper in the soul of a person must turn sour before he resorts to killing his self or abandoning all efforts to improve his lot.

Not all mentally ill, physically challenged, socially disadvantaged or tormented individuals consider suicide. Some people live and love more beautifully after a terrible ordeal or sickness. Conversely, not all suicidal persons are disabled or lacking. Many are privileged, youthful and highly intelligent.

The difference lies in the soul. Suicidal thinking may be a symptom of any number of psychological or medical conditions, but it is always also on some level a symptom of soul.

We give up when we lose sight of love, when we no longer believe in ourselves, others and God. When we are no longer able to see the goodness in ourselves, others and God, we lose heart, we lose the will to live. This loss of hope, vision and heart is due to the fact that the eye of our soul has gone dim. We have lost our true self, gone astray from God and broken our relationship to all that is beautiful, loving and true. In suicidal states the darkness of pain becomes our constant companion; we unwittingly wed ourselves to negativity and chain our hearts to despair, and thus make it nearly impossible for us to participate in goodness and grace.

It is not that goodness and grace are nonexistent, but that we merely lose sight of them. The interior lamp of the soul goes dim through neglect or self-abuse, or when it is overcome by the shadows of a confused, imperfect or painful outer reality. The soul grows weak through lack of love, wisdom and faith. Failure, sin, anger, greed, fear, pride, regret, criticism and a thousand other blemishes can tarnish the soul's original brilliance.

The reality of the soul is, at birth, bright and clear, and the truth of our being in God is always perfectly whole. However, we lose touch with that reality, and if we have any thought of returning to this original innocence, we are often blocked by feelings of unworthiness or the fear of appearing to be fools. Or we don't know where to start. Or we are afraid of getting our hopes up again. Or we shun anything that sounds too religious or spiritual. These thoughts make it difficult for us to see ourselves as we really are. If we had any idea of how perfectly loved, infinitely pure and desperately beautiful our souls were we would never become self-destructive.

Becoming Attached to Sickness

Sometimes it is easier to remain sick than it is to become whole. Thomas Aquinas wrote, "The soul is an uninhabited world that comes to life only when God lays his head against us."[1] God is always trying to "lay his head" upon us, but we don't let him. When he gets close we resist because we'd rather not change or we mistrust the whole notion of "God" and all that is associated with it.

There are times when we resist grace because we just don't feel worthy of being forgiven or healed. St. Teresa of Avila writes, "A thousand souls hear his call every second, but most every one then looks into their life's mirror and says, 'I am not worthy to leave this sadness.'"[2]

It's odd but true that it is very hard to leave our sadness behind. Sorrow is familiar territory. Psychologists talk of "secondary gain" to refer to the way in which our illnesses provide an unconscious benefit. Sometimes being sick is an escape from something we wish to avoid, or it causes others to take care of us. It may seem much more comfortable to remain helpless, dependent and weak than it is to have to face the world as an independent, strong and responsible individual. The benefits of being sick can be so seductively pleasurable that it becomes nearly impossible to give them up.

It requires true grace to break this chain. I cannot free myself of my neurotic attachments, aversions and illusions apart from divine intervention. "Divine intervention," or the advent of grace, allows me to transform my world, but it requires a bit of cooperation and some effort on my part. We must be willing to relinquish some control and to reexamine our being in relation to the world. Grace cannot fill us as long as we remain full of our self, that is, full of our attachments, aversions and illusions. Although the suffering that arises in relation to this self-centered world makes us miserable, at least it is familiar and known. To refuse to move from our familiar habitat is a bit like the baby eaglet that prefers to stay in the cramped nest of sticks and briers long after it is capable of flying. The grace that allows us to break our ego-bound attachments comes in a form much like that of the mother eagle who pushes and prods her young over the edge and into the abyss. Our suffering is God's way of nudging us to give up, let go and soar through the sky. Our minds and hearts have not yet discovered our innate ability to fly.

Troubles are life's way of prodding us forward. It is God's way of trying to "lay his head upon us" in order to make us whole so that we may fly just as we were born to do. We must learn to read the signs and hear God calling, acknowledging there is no need for fear when we are being pushed beyond our limits. This is the "cooperation" required of grace, that we accept God's will, looking in faith for the meaning in these troubled times and believing that the love of God calls us from and through our misery. In a remarkable way the eaglet is being called to exert very little effort other than to trust the mother's push and to open the wings it already has. The resistance is what interferes with the flying: the fear of change, the clinging to old ways, the failure to trust one's innate capacity to ride the wind.

Conversion from our self-reliant, egocentric, soul-sick condition is the only hope, not only for those suffering suicidal despair, but for all of us. Historically, persons who have been awakened at the deepest levels of their souls have been called mystics, and those who have discovered the joy and liberation of selflessness and grace have been called saints.

The Antidepressant Properties of Soul

According to the mystics and saints of every tradition and culture, the realization of one's "true self," the recovery of one's soul in God, has profound antidepressant properties. St. Francis de Sales wrote, "...a vigorous and resolute soul may live in the world without being infected with any of its moods."[3] Similarly, St. Paul said the spiritually awakened soul is characterized as one who is "afflicted in every way, but not crushed; perplexed, but not driven to despair;...struck down, but not destroyed."[4] The "fruit" of a spiritually awakened soul is "love, joy, peace, patience, kindness, goodness, faithfulness, gentleness and self-control," all the properties of heart and mind that contradict the disabling effects of hatred, despair, hopelessness and defeat.[5] Conversely, according to Thomas Merton, "Turbulence of spirit is a sign of spiritual weakness."[6]

There is much truth to these sayings. This leads to the fairly easily drawn conclusion that suicidal depression and despair are the cries of the soul and that soul treatment can often induce the sort of healing that is needed. Granted, there are times when soul care cannot break through until a person is medicated, hospitalized or treated physically, but other times soul work may be all that is needed.

With the recovery of one's soul comes the opening of the spiritual eye. When the eye of the soul is opened, life appears altogether different. Suffering is transformed. Love is everywhere. Grace abounds. Spiritually awakened persons recognize, as Jean-Pierre de Caussade put it, that "everything is significant, and everything makes perfect sense."[7] There are no mistakes, all is within the divinely unfolding providential will of the Father of all created things and beings. We are never alone. We are never apart from the greater good of grace. There is always hope and help. We are never abandoned or rejected by life.

You may be able to identify a time in the past when God was there for you. Or, more recently, you may be able to recognize the hand of God at work in your situation. Perhaps you would have already killed yourself if it were not for some "coincidence." Angels come in many disguises and often go unrecognized. A friend might call. We might have a sudden feeling or memory. Our children may come to us just as we are about to overdose. An important magazine article or book may appear at the right time. The gun we planned to use may come up strangely missing, or it fails to fire. A neighbor calls the police. These are remarkably common occurrences in stories of suicide attempts that have failed. In all these things and more, we are being whispered to by the "angels," and everything is working in our behalf in an effort to call us back from the edge. In a thousand ways we are being nurtured, encouraged and invited to grow and live rather than die.

Unbeknown to us, behind every misfortune, mishap, mistake and miserable circumstance there lies a hidden grace. People of faith "enjoy supreme bliss because they see the fullness of God's power being exercised in whatever conditions of body or soul they find themselves, in whatever happens to them internally or externally and in whatever befalls them at each and every moment. The soul, with its living faith in God, always sees him acting behind happenings which bewilder our senses."[8] Within all of our circumstances and pains, we are told by the masters of the faith, there is this working of grace, leading and protecting and perfecting us as we are willing.

Grace Is Already Here

Grace is always here. Just as the natural "space" surrounding and embracing our body in this very instant simultaneously extends into the outer reaches of infinite space, without our ever giving it any thought, so infinite grace is always surrounding us. Like oxygen, grace is always available and active, yet it remains out of our awareness even as we breathe it in. In another way, grace may be likened to the radio waves that are constantly surrounding us. So long as we have our tuners off, or we're tuned into the chatter and clatter of some other noise, we will hear no music. It doesn't mean the music is not there.

Grace is everywhere. If it were not so we would already be dead. We would have never been born. We would have never had one moment of peace or love or beauty. The oxygen in our air would turn to poisonous gas, and our pores would close in upon us without grace. It is easy to notice what is wrong with our lives, like seeing only the one dark stain on a pure white tablecloth, but in searching for signs of grace we must notice how much of the cloth is clean and white.

If we could see beyond our unfortunate circumstances, we would see a shroud of goodness protecting and supporting us at every turn. For certain, there is plenty of misfortune and loss, but even in those times there is grace, sometimes more than in times of pleasure and ease.

For instance, it is nearly impossible to see much of anything when we are in a dark time. In addition, we have all been conditioned to see things according to our upbringing and training. We see only what we pay attention to. It is impossible to see spiritual realities until the eye of the soul is opened, and the spiritual eye will not open without our consent.

So much of our energies is spent on shutting down the eye of truth. We shut out pain. We shut out the realization of what we are doing to others and ourselves. We look away from opportunities to heal, to forgive, to recover and to find joy. We lock ourselves in our rooms. We avoid others. We refuse to take our medication or to give up our addictions. We look only in the direction of our preconceived perceptions or focus our attention exclusively on our losses and pains. We see only ourselves, what we lack or what we want. We close our hearts to the truth.

Moments of grace and gift escape our attention every day. Every one of us has been beaten down, rained on and unfairly disadvantaged, but we have also been loved, led, fed, clothed, gifted and protected in more ways than we will ever know.

Infinity is forever a promise and potentiality, but more so, it is a constant companion and present reality. This infinity is within us and around us. No matter how constricted and closed off we may feel, we are never far from grace. We fail to see this "infinite" reality because the doors of our perception have been negatively affected by our self-interest and doubt, anger and regret, greed and fear.

A story from the Gospels relates how Peter walked on the rough seas toward Jesus. He stayed above water as long as he held his eyes on the infinite, but as soon as he looked down at the physical, that is, the concrete, discrete and time-bound realities of the waves and water, he sunk like a brick.

Suicide becomes an option when we are deeply wounded but are too soul-blind to see the healing grace, the Jesus figure, walking on the surface of our troubles and moving right toward us. We fail to see when we shut our eyes or when the circumstances cloud and confuse the images. Even the followers of Christ who were visited by him following his resurrection were given an image that was difficult to discern. They thought he was the gardener or a ghost and not a real manifestation. Some who saw still did not believe because their hearts were closed. Yet, those who had the eyes to see, the faith to see, the willingness to see truly saw. Their eyes were opened and they saw him through his many disguises.

Opening the Soul's Eye

How do we open the eye of our soul?

Brother Lawrence's formula seems best; he says, "I have set myself simply and solely to know and love God himself, and to renounce all substitutes and formulas—even religious ones."[9] As the mystics explain it, God cannot be apprehended by the intellect or reason. He is "known" by a direct and immediate experience that cannot be adequately described or conveyed in words or thought. If God is sought with abandon and singleness of heart, with an utter desperation and in faith, he will manifest, regardless of how unworthy, unprepared or ignorant we are. In fact, God makes himself knowable only to those who look for him and expect to find him. It is a very strange business, this thing of "knowing" God, but he "draws nigh" to those who draw nigh to him, and remains hidden for those who fail to seek.

It may be helpful for some to consider that the God to which I refer here is not the God of my understanding or of your childhood or even of the greatest theologians and philosophers. It is the God beyond all understanding, interpretations and representations. An intellectual knowledge of God is beyond our mental capabilities, but in the time-honored words of the writer of the sixteenth-century classic, *The Cloud of Unknowing*, "God can only be known by love, never the mind."[10] I like that. I think it's closer to the truth than any other idea as to how one can "know" a Being who is clearly beyond human comprehension. We can't understand God, but we can learn to love him, and in that longing to know him by love we call him out from his apparent obscurity into the light of understanding in the depths of our very own hearts.

The truth, being, power and reality that exist in God, behind all our images of God, are most certain. But our ideas about God are always partial. Our previous training, images, perceptions and thoughts about God have always been incomplete, since "God" is by definition beyond human comprehension. We can only begin to approach the one true God by leaving behind all thought and reaching out in bare attention and love. We will talk more of this as we go along, but for a more complete description of some practical tips and a fuller description of how to approach God in love without reliance on thought, I recommend James Finley's book, *Christian Meditation*.[11]

God is "discovered" only when he chooses to reveal himself to us, and he reveals himself only to those who approach him in love, brokenness and humility. This is good news to those of us despairing of our lives because brokenness is something we are already quite familiar with, and love is something we already have and have need of all the more. The one true grace is an active, vital presence beyond all religious ceremony, dogmatic beliefs or traditional forms. God is a person. This God is not scared by failure, sin, imperfection and doubt. God does not resist or ridicule the lost soul floundering in darkness, but rather calls out to it all the more during times of crisis and despair. This God does not expect perfection, right theology or a particular ritual of approach. The one true God of grace is open, receptive and available to anyone who approaches with a true and humble heart.

Grace is not some new theory, nor is it some "thing" we can manipulate through intellectual understanding or earn by virtue of our will power, experience or pedigree. It is not some magical antidote to despair that the medical, intellectual or scientific community can simply hand out. Nor is it possible to present a scientific proof of the reality of grace.

What matters most is not how we interpret grace but how we approach it. We cannot attack it, force it or manipulate it, but we can open ourselves to it. We can prepare our hearts, invite it in, clear a space for it and look expectantly for its appearance. We can entice it in by acting gracefully toward others and our selves, as the more grace we give the more we will receive. We can open our hearts to it and we can recognize the ways in which we may have overlooked, blocked or doubted it in the past. There are no "easy" solutions, but there are solutions. There is a process whereby all lost and confounded things, like the grass in winter, can grow their way back up into the light.

CHAPTER 6
Damage Control

The suicide expert Edwin Shneidman wrote, "Never kill yourself while you are suicidal."[1] That may sound unusual at first, but what he means is that when suicide seems to be a reasonable solution, that is the very time that you can be sure you are not reasoning with a healthy mind. Suicide is the desperate plan of a desperate brain. The troubled mind's biggest mistake is to confuse a temporary problem with a permanent one, and then to apply a permanent solution to a temporary concern. We do not push our car over a cliff because the battery has gone dead, but you would be shocked at how often a person tries to kill himself when a relatively minor and short-term problem troubles him.

Among the experts it is known that suicidal people are characterized by this narrowness of thought and constricted vision. The nature of depression, pessimism and negativity causes one to focus exclusively on what cannot be done, to see only the problem and to miss the solution. Optimists and survivors, on the other hand, always seem to think the answer is just around the corner, and their belief makes it so.

We are all prone to lose faith from time to time. Losers and quitters are characterized by a loss of faith, an inability to see into the next inning and to visualize a hit instead of another strikeout. Winners, however, are known for their capacity to see the previously unrecognized opportunities, hidden options and undiscovered connections. They can "see" a positive outcome.

Usually, in a James Bond movie, the villain gets cornered, freezes and is killed. However, when Bond is cornered, he always finds the unforeseen avenue of escape. The magic behind Bond's survival is not so much in his brute strength but in his ability to believe that he can and will escape. Of course, Bond is a fantasy, but in real life there are those people who are the equivalent to Bond in that they find themselves in impossible emotional and spiritual dilemmas but are just as adept as Bond at averting a tragic outcome regardless of the odds.

Whenever I try one of those mind puzzler games, there always comes a moment when I think, "This is impossible." When I remember that it can be done and I have seen it done by others, I am reinvigorated and inspired again to go at it with renewed zeal. So often in our confusion we forget to remember that it is possible for the human spirit to endure insurmountable pain, impossible odds and inconceivable torments. It happens every day.

Sometimes the answer is right in front of us or is about to become apparent within the next five minutes or five days, but we are so impatient. A woman I recently saw tried to kill herself by overdose three times within a month. I pointed out to her that it would take longer to recover from a broken arm than she was allowing herself to recover from her broken heart. It makes no sense and is extremely unfair to ourselves to expect that we must recover from a major setback, loss or disappointment sooner than the milk in our refrigerator expires.

If impatience does not get us, thoughtless frenetic activity will. At times we become so panic-stricken that we jump from one conclusion to the next, alternating directions and swapping out reactions like a drunken sailor in a squall. Our boat is pitching, kicking and stalling, then flipping violently in the opposite direction. The rigging is whipping and the mainsail slams across the center of the boat, nearly decapitating us. We don't know whether we should steer into the wind, away from it or to the side. We can no longer tell which direction the wind blows or where we are headed. Yet we continue to push and pull at the lines, fighting the rudder this way and that, when all we need to do is let go and drop sail, stop struggling against the wind and tide, and ride it out until things quiet down and we gain our bearings.

Another common mistake is to become trapped in an "all or nothing" solution-focused strategy. Sometimes we are caught up in the wrongheaded fallacy that we cannot survive unless we have one particular answer. Frequently suicidal individuals tell me they cannot live without their girlfriend or boyfriend or their father's acceptance or whatever else it is they imagine to be their only reason to live.

In our confused state we sometimes insist on a solution that is impossible or illogical. This sort of hardheaded, single-minded insistence on one particular solution is an important contributor to feeling trapped.

For instance, if your wife has left you and is already in love with someone else, has taken out restraining orders against you and has divorce papers filed, you are only locking yourself into certain failure if you insist that you cannot and will not go on with your life without her. Of course, a miracle may happen, and you may try to talk to her when the opportunity arises, but for you to continue to insist that you cannot live until or unless she changes her mind is to paint yourself into a corner.

I like to remind people of the barefooted man who came to the guru. He complained that his feet were very sore and that he had exhausted all his income and energy in trying to place carpeting over all the places he needed to go. He was desperate and exhausted, saying his life had become hopelessly restricted and painful. The guru simply gave him a pair of sandals, and the man was free to walk freely wherever he wanted, pain-free. In almost every case of suicidal desperation, there is a solution that has not yet dawned on us. Like the man in the story, it is not from a lack of effort that we have been so narrowly focused on how to solve this particular riddle that we have missed the obvious. Also like the man in our story, so many of us try to soften the entire world by insisting and wishing that everyone and everything else operate fairly and smoothly, rather than changing the things within our self that will better prepare us for the rocky road ahead.

Slow Down and Wait for a Solution

Sometimes we need to calm down and relax into a solution. Like a drowning man who thrashes against a lifeguard's attempts to pull him in, our fear sometimes causes us to kick and fight against our own savior, making it impossible to see that we are already being supported and drawn to safety. Or it may be that we can actually swim if we made a proactive attempt at trying to stay above water rather than fighting so hard against drowning.

Meditation, quiet self-reflection and time alone can all be very critical in times of crisis, but most of us have a tendency to run from one person to the next, to move from one fix to another, to rely on the external and more apparent forms of power, while ignoring the quiet voice of inner wisdom that whispers which way to go, offering assurance and support. When our forces are scattered we cannot really hear these whispers, and then we are unable to decide which "answers" are false and insubstantial and which are worthy of our attention.

What may help us most is often within our grasp if we would stop long enough to see it or wait long enough for it to arrive. They that "wait upon the LORD," says Isaiah, they are the ones who will "renew their strength," they will "mount up with wings like eagles, they shall run and not be weary, they shall walk and not faint."[2] "Be still and know that I am God" is yet another admonition from God given in the Psalms, yet how often really do we ever stop, wait and become still when we are emotionally distraught?[3] We don't wait or stop long enough to see if God will come through because we are too busy running about trying to fix things through our own power.

This is especially true for addicts, who are so often numbered among the suicidal. They arrive at the emergency department week after week, sick and homeless, disgusted at their drug-induced behaviors and wanting to die. Yet they are so afraid of giving up the booze or drug that they hang on to the very thing that is pulling them under while they look for something besides sobriety to improve their plight. Stop and listen to your heart, listen to your life and see if you can't discover what it is that is really pulling you down.

We must widen the angle and consider anything and everything as a potential solution. Often the solution is simple, but so much of the time what is simple is not easy, and often what becomes so complicated to us is made impossible by our own twisted reasoning or habitual determination to find only one way through this experience.

There Is a Way from Here to There

The way out of any wilderness is always "through" it. There will be more confusion and struggle before there is relief. Even when we are on the "perfect" trail out of the woods, we will encounter many more thickets and briers on the way out. We must remember, however, that we are indeed on the way as long as we keep moving and trying different paths.

One option that is sure to fail is refusing to walk down any new path until we are assured it is the right one. We are not always sure, and most of the time we have to make a move based on partial information, hints or pure intuition. Standing still is important at first, to get our bearings and make a plan, maybe to pray for guidance or to get our sense of direction. Then we must act. We cannot wait for a total solution before we take a risk and move.

In every forest there is a way out, a path that leads home. We just have to find it, and finding it may take some trial and error. We may have to go down some frustrating trails and circle about before we get our bearings, but we will never get our bearings by standing still and waiting for that one revelation, the perfect approach or a complete assurance of the proper direction. It does not normally come that way, even when God is showing you the way out. He typically starts by merely pointing you in the right direction or offering a small clearing in the thicket. There are no guarantees or blaring street signs at this stage.

A tiny glimpse of the way is enough to start. As you move, new information becomes available. This is hard for those who lack vision or faith, because most of the time the very first steps in the right direction have to be chosen in faith. We don't know when we start out if our efforts will pay off, but we must start just the same. All great accomplishments and successes start out with a vision, a mere thought that is believed in but not proven or actually seen with the naked eye. The future is seen by faith.

There are no absolutes, and some of our initial attempts will be wrong, but these false starts are necessary also. The dead ends tell us where not to go next time. Thomas Edison reportedly said, after having failed a hundred or more times to find the right filament for his lightbulb, that he had not failed a hundred times, but had rather ruled out so many wrong filaments that the right one was surely to be that much closer to becoming evident.

One definition of character neurosis is repeating behaviors that do not work. It would be like Edison trying to use tin foil fifty more times after he had already established it would not work. Or it would be like you trying to get over your depression through drinking after finding that the alcohol use had just made things worse, and then drinking to try and forget about it all over again.

We scream at our kids to make them behave and they get more agitated, so we scream louder and longer, never thinking of taking a completely different approach. This is all too familiar. We have to change our approach, our circumstances, our attitude or all three of them if we are to have any chance of success. We must begin to recognize which of our strategies are failing and replace them with others that may have a better chance of working.

We must never give up. When we are lost in the woods, we must remember that there are streets and cities, open fields and vast expanses of sea and sky that are merely out of our sight at this moment. They do exist, and we can get to them from where we are. But we must believe and hope and act.

There is no room for giving up after realizing that the first few paths have led us deeper into the woods. If we stop trying different paths we will surely die in the woods. This describes the suicidal state of mind. If we are trying, even faulty weak misled steps can lead us to where we need to go. Every weak and faltering step changes the scenery, opening up new vistas, offering new glimpses of other trails we have not yet seen.

We cannot overlook the value of small steps. When everything in our life is trying to shut us down, every step is an act of courage and defiance against the oppressive wilderness of doubt and defeat. In trying to dispel darkness, the darker it is, the greater the impact even the tiniest spark of light can have.

Take Inventory

It is important to examine what you have been doing so far to help yourself. You may not have considered your actions or lack of activity as a "strategy," but it is. If it has not been a consciously developed plan, it is a strategy adopted by default. Most of what we do when we are stressed is automatic. Without thinking we react in our habitual way. Whatever we have relied on in the past becomes our default mode of dealing, and that particular form of defense may be the worst possible strategy in this instance. Whatever you are currently doing or refusing to do is your way of dealing with or refusing to deal with your problems. Ask yourself if your current approach is working.

Some of us get angry at everything and everybody but ourselves, while others take all the blame and bad feeling into themselves whether it is their fault or not. Some of us overeat, oversleep, drink too much or work too much in an effort to avoid our feelings at any cost. Others stay awake for days obsessing over every emotional detail. Some run mindlessly to books and parents and friends seeking direction from everyone but themselves. Still others isolate and refuse to get any help from anyone. Sometimes we pretend our problems do not exist and at other times we exaggerate them beyond reason. We run to God expecting some magical intervention, or else we refuse to pray or believe there is any possibility of divine help.

Extremes in any one direction will almost always fail us. Notice what your tendency is and consider doing the opposite. If you have been taking it all on yourself, call on someone else to help you. If you think all your troubles are someone else's responsibility, look for what part you have to play. If you are always angry, learn to forgive. If you are always making excuses for the ones who hurt you, use your anger to assert your right to be safe and free of abuse. Take a cue from your excesses. If you have let everything fall apart, begin straightening up. If you are obsessively concerned about having everything perfect, learn to loosen up and make some mistakes. Everything is a matter of balance.

It seems that many suicidal people are overly serious. Often there seems to be a lack of humor and perspective, an overreliance on perfectionism and brute strength. Strength and perfection are certainly ideal, but these do not reside in us alone. Nor can they always be relied on or called up at will. It is not always perfection or power that gets us through. Sometimes beauty, flow, creativity and acceptance are just as critical. Everything in retrospect will look differently.

We may look back in a few years and wonder how we ever thought Sharon with the doe eyes in eighth grade was the only girl in the world. We might remember those weeks we spent in jail after having stolen a car on a dare and now laugh. In the midst of these experiences we can easily feel desperate and even desirous of death, seeing only the bars of the cell. Isn't it so true that life is a tragic comedy, that there is a sad, happy, crazy wonder in it all and that given time we can almost always look back and see our tragedies with perspective and a lighter touch?

As we lose this perspective, we fall back on a humorless and grim approach. We expect a lot and then try harder, but the fact is that we may be trying too hard or expecting too much. Like one of those Chinese finger puzzles made of interwoven straw that slips on our fingers, the more we rely on brute force and the harder we pull in the direction that seems most logical, the tighter the finger trap gets. Sometimes we have to give up, stop trying, let go and push in the opposite direction before our knotted lives can become untangled.

Part of our challenge is to discover which of our attempts at finding a way through the pain have failed, and then to discern which ones have failed because they are bad ideas and which ones simply haven't had time to work yet. With the passage of time, things will become clear, so one of the most important things to give yourself in times of despair is time.

Refuse to Act in Haste

You can kill yourself. No one can stop you. Police and hospitals and therapists can slow you down, but no one can keep you from it if that is what you are determined to do. Slowing you down, however, is a significant step in helping you change your mind. You may have been thinking suicide is a great solution, but if you are like most, you will think differently in a day or two.

Hundreds of thousands have tried to kill themselves and failed. Although many of them succeed with a subsequent attempt, the majority of persons who have made a suicidal gesture or attempt and lived through it later change their minds. With intervention and time, and sometimes even the smallest improvement in their situations, many come to feel that they are very glad they didn't succeed in killing themselves.

One man I know cut his throat, tried overdosing a couple times and held a gun to his head more than once. Now, seven years down the road, his life has changed, and he thanks God every day for not allowing his "temporary insanity" to kill him during a hard but temporary period of bad luck. Another person whom I know jumped from a very high bridge, but some tree branches broke his fall in such a way that he was banged up but escaped death. Many others have died from the same jump. He says he will never do anything like that again, and he cannot believe now he even did it.

If you have tried suicide or are thinking about it but still have doubts about truly ending your life, you are fortunate. That doubt is your greatest friend and your best wisdom. The small voice of doubt in your heart of hearts is the "self" that knows you will eventually come into a better way.

This self is the "Self of the universe," the voice of life working still in your deepest core being. It is your true being united with life's relentless urge to create, grow and express its most intimate secrets. It is being that is soul. You might think of it as the inner child, the poet inside who died young, the innocent victim of all the maddening chaos buzzing about you and in your head. This "true self," buried now beneath a pile of broken dreams and heartache, is still wise and strong. It is a survivor and fighter because it knows things about life that your confused self has forgotten or may have never really comprehended.

Your true being understands failure and pain. It does not understand the why of it any more than your confused outer shell, but it accepts it all and never gives up. Like an old forgotten tulip bulb in winter, it just keeps on living beneath the surface, in the darkened damp, with no signs of blooming in sight.

Life will never undermine itself. Therefore we can be sure that whatever voices inside us that tell us suicide is a good idea are the voices of death and evil. God, his angels, your lost loved ones and even your true being will never encourage suicide.

Life supports life. The life force inside you sees the future and intuits the meaning of the mysteries of existence that baffle you so. Your soul can see what you can no longer see when you're clouded by anger, grief, sadness and anxiety. It is telling you to hold off on suicide.

If you were going to buy a car, you certainly would not want to do it when you were stone drunk at a convention of used car salespersons. You would want to be as clear as possible, compare models and get away from all the pitches before deciding even something this minor. In deciding to take one's own life, an individual needs to be thinking clearly and have all the facts. Get some sleep, sober up, take your medication, contemplate all the angles, consult family, pray about it or try and sit still for a day or two.

Suicide may look good now because death is the best of all lying salesmen. However, the voice of doubt is in the light; it is telling you the truth.

This Too Will Pass

It may be helpful to realize that suicidal thoughts, feelings, gestures and attempts arrive in little pockets of time, explode and then subside. They are episodic and periodic. One who is suicidal is very rarely suicidal every day or even every hour. There comes a brief window of time in which one is suicidal and then it is gone.

Contrary to popular belief and in contradiction to the frustration emergency workers often feel toward people who seem to make multiple halfhearted suicide attempts yet call for help or arrange to be found, many people want to die and want to be rescued at the same time. We can feel both things simultaneously. Just like when you are on a diet and want to raid the refrigerator yet avoid it at the same time, these individuals are torn. They don't know what they want. They want both to die and to be helped. This confusion, this dilemma is very real. They are not just manipulating the system or looking for attention. These individuals are conflicted, scared, tired and desperate. Death looks like an easy way out and a nightmare all at once. They want to disappear but not die. Maybe they wish to fall asleep and never wake up but are terrified of the pain and uncertainty of death. They want to be saved but doubt it is possible.

This is frequently the case in suicide "attempts" that fail. The person is not committed to death but is flirting with it. Unfortunately, many such halfhearted people die even when they are not sure they want to be dead. Conversely, many who are extremely serious and intent on killing themselves survive and become worse later on. Many are found too late with, in cases of hanging, evidence of scratch marks around the noose, or over-dosers may try to regurgitate their pills and die on the vomit. Perhaps even worse are the ones who survive violent attempts such as gunshot wounds or jumps from high places. Many live but are permanently brain damaged, physically disabled or horribly disfigured. I know one such woman who threw herself in front of a train and now lives the life of an invalid.

Make the commitment to live. Learn to wait. Listen to the voice of doubt because it comes from your wisest center. It includes subconscious thought, subliminal memories, archaic symbolism from dreams and fragments of perhaps a larger intelligence such as God or your ancestors.

Patience makes use of the time you have, and it can withstand anything. Patience is the soul's best friend. It requires no amount of effort and costs nothing. It takes no special skill or training. All you can do sometimes is wait. Let go of all efforts, sit without resistance or anxious longing and wait. Do nothing until you know what to do. Allow all the sorrow and despair of your current condition to flow over you like the currents of a river over a stone. Sit like that stone.

You cannot drown in this flood. It cannot kill you or carry you away or make you do anything.

As long as we can sit and patiently wait, we will be safe, and the flood will pass. When we do not know what to believe anymore, we don't have to believe anything. When we don't know what to do, it's okay to do nothing. It's all right to not believe in or act on the good, as long as we also refrain from acting on and believing in destruction.

Everything changes. Some of it will get worse; some will go away; some new factors will come into play. Fortune will smile and frown its way through each life, but as long as we remain at the center of the wheel we will not be tossed up and down with its ever-changing cycles.

There is an old teaching illustration called the *Wheel of Fortune*. It was an illustration of a great wheel, like a Ferris wheel at a carnival, representing life going around and around, up and down, ever spinning its course. On the outer rim of this wheel are pictured clowns, some hanging on to the rim, smiling as the wheel ascends. Others are falling in terror off the other side as the wheel of fortune turns. The smiling ones are only a half-turn from going down as their fortunes change.[4] The important teaching in this illustration is in showing how the wisest persons remained at the center of the hub, in equanimity, no longer tossed up and down on the ever-changing fortunes of life. By remaining at the center, at the soul of things, we no longer need be tossed up and down. The changing fortunes of existence will never stop moving up and down, around and around, but we can change ourselves in relation to it by placing ourselves silently in the center, watching and waiting.

Stay safe, stay centered and wait in that secret place inside yourself where you are resting in the changeless hub.

CHAPTER 7
The Role of Adversity

Losses on the external and temporal plane can either send us off in a thousand different directions, scattering our energies to the wind, or they can direct us straight back to our hearts and to God. If we are fortunate, pain and loss will lead us inward, to our true self in God. If we allow our pain to direct us into our heart, we may find that God is there, accomplishing his greatest work in and through us. In that moment when we feel as if God has forsaken us, as Christ himself felt on the cross, we may actually be closer to his perfect will than ever before, just as Christ was when he was being offered up as sacrifice in the sacred fire of God's all-consuming love. Crucifixion, in God's story for us, is as it was for Christ, not a tragic end, but an unavoidable passage on the way to the resurrection.

Suffering has its meaning. When we forget this and allow our suffering to drive us to anger, fear, blame, shame and regret, we stay on our crosses and in our tombs. There can be no resurrection without love and the remembrance of God.

When we lose sight of God's love, we go against our loss and pain. Like a deer caught in a barbed-wire fence, we tear ourselves to pieces fighting back. We move further from the truth of who we are and become more angry and frustrated with every kick. Failures, faults, wounds and losses hurt very badly, and there is no way of avoiding a great deal of it, so it is imperative to remember that these things are not there to kill us. They may be there to kill our willfulness or ignorance but not our soul.

Adversity reproduces in us a crop of goodness. Like pruning back a fruit tree, the snipping away is meant to bring forth something beautiful, something not yet ripe in us. All that God wants to bring forth in us is love, and the fruit of love, multiplying his gentleness toward us and filling us with his sweet nectar.

God is most intent on finding his way into our hearts when we are most wounded. Just as the prodigal son's father allowed his child to take his inheritance and leave home to squander it on reckless living, God leaves us to our foolishness but then comes racing in our direction the moment we realize our mistakes and begin the journey back home. As writer Paul Evdokimov put it, "The brutal experience of our falls and weakness can fling us to the edge of despair...[but] God is watching for us at this decisive moment."[1]

When depression, lack, brokenness and suicidal thoughts take us to the edge of despair, God is there waiting for us. The soul's primary role in times of despair is to allow us to see that this is true, to remind us of it and to help us find God hidden there among the brambles and shambles of our broken life. Among spiritual adepts these consistent themes appear regarding the role of human suffering: all suffering is meant to drive us back to God; all heartache originates in our homesickness for God; all failure is to remind us of our dependence on God. Ignorance intensifies the suffering, and the darkest night is merely setting the stage for the coming dawn.

Jesus said it is the sick that are in need of a physician, suggesting that anyone who fails to recognize how truly sick they are will never be healed by the Great Physician. Without pain we don't know we are sick, and when we don't know it, we avoid the cure and remain sick until it is too late. Glaucoma is one such disease that has no painful symptoms. The pressure inside the diseased eye can slowly build and destroy the retinal nerve, making the person blind before she even knows anything is wrong.

Furthermore, Jesus said, "Blessed are those who hunger and thirst for righteousness, for they will be filled." *Blessed* means "happy." "Blessed are those who mourn, for they will be comforted. Blessed are the poor in spirit, for theirs is the kingdom of heaven."[2] Dare we imagine that, in saying this, Jesus was also implying that those who never weep or mourn or find themselves driven by intense starvation and thirst will never be able to be blessed, happy, comforted, satisfied or filled with God?

Learning the Greatest Lessons

Logic tells us discomfort is "bad," but soul logic tells us that our negative experiences, unwanted losses, irritating neighbors and difficult emotions are our teachers. They grant us opportunities to develop patience, to discover new things about ourselves and to learn how to go to God when we are too sick and scared to help ourselves. Nothing is lost, wasted or mistakenly allowed to fall into our path. Everything has a purpose and is allowed by God in order to perfect us in love. Like the pressures and digs of a master potter as he molds and shapes the clay on his wheel, so the bending and breaking of our wills and hearts form and transform us, shaping our useless and "uninhabited" lumps of clay into vessels of beauty and usefulness. Negative experiences enlarge our capacity to love and be loved, if we allow ourselves to stay on the wheel and be molded and changed by them.

One way adversity attempts to enlarge the soul is to spoil our taste for anything less than God. When we are young and foolish we think a hot new car or a big promotion will fix our lives or that if things could always go our way we would be happy. However, as we mature we learn that these things are not true or possible. Adversity shatters our illusions of finding true and lasting fulfillment through any form of addiction, attachment, illusion, possession, pleasure or achievement. It breaks apart the false imagination that we have all grown up with, namely, that we will eventually be able to perfect ourselves enough to become whole and content through our own efforts. Adversity brings us face to face with our own smallness, selfishness and morbidity. We learn that we cannot do it all, we cannot please everyone, we cannot perfect ourselves, we cannot control everything and we may now be discovering we cannot even find our way back home. We are pressed to the edge of our own resources and are forced to either learn about gift and grace, or give up.

Through the lessons of our adversity, we discover that there is no place to hide. Everything is falling apart, fleeting, insubstantial, illusory and unsatisfactory. We are steeped in insecurity. We are born alone and we will die alone. If we are fortunate, we will become disillusioned with everything the world, the flesh, the devil and the ego have to offer so that we learn to let it all go. We let the ego-centered self go. We die to our own efforts and throw ourselves upon the mercy of God. Then our life can begin.

There is an old saying in Zen, restated concisely by singer songwriter Donovan Leach as, "…first there is a mountain, then there is no mountain, then there is." First we think the world might save us, then we think it never will, but then, after we are transformed by love, we recognize that the world does not have to save us at all, that we are complete within through our union with the transcendent All. Then we are free to return to the world awake and aware, centered and whole. We can walk its green hills without needing to buy the land, and we can hear its birds singing without trying to cage them. We can participate in the lives of others and help, without attachment to results or the need to control.

God sees our most difficult times as the best opportunity to get through to us. Like an ice water vendor in the desert, his cool, refreshing waters appeal to us most when we have reached the hottest and driest portion of our journey. Every soldier in the heat of battle thinks about God, even if it's for just one moment and even if he had been a professed atheist moments before the bombs began to fall around him. Adversity makes us thirsty for the One.

Thomas Moore says that care of the soul involves a "fundamentally different way of regarding daily life and the quest for happiness." He says soul care is a "continuous process that concerns itself not so much with 'fixing' a central flaw," but rather a way of taking those flaws and learning from them. Soul work is "not primarily a method of problem solving," but is rather a way to "be ready for the conflict of life." Care of the soul, then, "appreciates the mystery of human suffering" and looks upon suffering as "symptoms," symptoms of our greater illness, which is our loss of God and self. He suggests we can "find the messages that lie within the illness, the corrections that can be found in remorse and other uncomfortable feelings, and the necessary changes requested by depression and anxiety."[3]

John of the Cross, the sixteenth-century master of the soul's progress and development, describes a process whereby God actively attempts to "withdraw from us all sensory delight and pleasure," to give us "pure dryness and interior darkness" in order to "wean us from the breasts of these gratifications and delights," so that we may "set the eyes of faith on this invisible grace" and eventually enter into the sweetness and completion that is found in God alone.[4]

English Poet John Keats once put it this way, "Do you not see how necessary a World of Pains and troubles is to school an Intelligence and make it a soul?"[5] Intelligence, reason, ordinary awareness, all of which we have been referring to here as "ego," or the false self, becomes a "soul" through the teachings of pain and trouble. You may have known some people, as I have, who have a great deal of intelligence but no soul. Perfectly intelligent, beautiful, wealthy and healthy individuals can sometimes seem to be the ones with the least amount of soul. As I stated in one of my previous books, "…intelligence without heart is brainsickness."[6] Keats is not just suggesting it is a good idea to go through trouble and pain now and again in order to find your center, to make you into a "soul," but that it is an absolute necessity. It can happen no other way.

If we follow the trail of our own blood back to the place where we were most wounded, we will discover a great deal about soul. We will find the place where our greatest gifts can be born. The best addiction therapists are the ones who have themselves been torn apart by their own addictions. Those who have survived abuse or neglect as children are able to battle for the rights of children with a conviction and passion like no one else. Mothers who lose their sons to drunk drivers are the ones who start national campaigns against such stupidity. Social and political activists who have made the hugest differences on issues of racial justice, sexual equality, workers' rights, religious tolerance and more have been the ones who first tasted intolerance, abuse, injustice and inequality. There is gold in the dung heaps of our hurts if we have the courage to dig through the mess and pull it out.

Pain Is Not the Problem

Pain teaches us a lesson. Pain is not really the enemy. It is the resistance to and denial of legitimate pain that deadens the soul. Carl Jung said that all neurosis is an avoidance of legitimate suffering. He meant that what robs us of our humanity and sanity most is not suffering but our inability to accept it and make something of it. It is when we attempt to deny, hide from, avoid or justify legitimate pain that we hurt ourselves all the more. What we bury, we bury alive, and it will haunt us until we dig it up and face it squarely.

The avoidance of legitimate suffering is only a part of a larger avoidance with even greater consequences, and that is the avoidance or denial of things as they are. This fundamental denial is perhaps the core of all existential despair. It is an attempted escape from life. It is what keeps us from engaging life, and as we fail to understand or accept life as it actually is, life becomes increasingly chaotic and incomprehensible to us. One must always accept and understand things as they are. It must be a lifetime practice to return repeatedly to reality as it is, and this practice may in fact constitute the fundamental challenge of all contemplative soul work.

Happiness, sanity and the recovery from suicidal despair must always involve facing and accepting things as they are. Facing things as they are ultimately is a way of entering into what religion calls reality, truth and reunion with the One. While pain's duty is to help empty us of falsehood, ignorance, ego and separation from the One, this commitment to things as they are is our way back to the One. By ridding our false sense of security based on the ignorance and mistaken identity of the ego, pain brings us to the cusp of the absolute insecurity of emptiness which, according to the great mystic teachers, is the "fullness of the All that is."

Buddhists talk of the realization of "emptiness" and "selflessness," which permits us to see past our separate identity into what we really are, in and as a manifestation of the whole, returning us to our True Self, sometimes referred to as our Original Face or Buddha Nature. In Christianity the words are different, but the meaning is much the same. We are lost from God in sin, banished from the garden of union with God and wandering about in a life of alienation and separation from the One. Christ comes to abolish sin and remove the barrier between our old, false self and the One, thus reuniting us to God so that we may be one with the Father as he is One with the Father, returning us to our original and true identity in God.

It may be that the life you think you have lost and have been trying to recover was merely a life of illusion and mischief. When we let go of our small "s" *self* and discover something more about our fulfillment and true identity in God, we will not be left with nothingness or mere speculative philosophy but with love. The emptiness, the union, the One, the true self; these are all metaphors for love.

In a beautiful and clarifying verse, Stephen Batchelor writes, "To experience emptiness (i.e., selflessness) is not a descent into the abyss of nothingness nor an ascent into a separate realm. It is a recovery of the freedom to configure oneself in the intentional, unimpeded trajectory through the shifting, ambiguous sands of life. To recognize this emptiness is not a negation of life: it gives us a glimpse of what enables anything to happen at all."[7] In other words, pain rips apart ego's false moorings to a shifting and unstable world so that it can become free to move among the sublime freedom of grace in, not apart from, the world of pain by participation in it through the true self. Emptiness, then, is a realization of the emptiness of ego and the false self, which is an opening into the true self and the egoless state of God, which is the love in us, right where we are.

When a man has been shot with an arrow, asking questions about who shot him, what type of arrow it was, why he was targeted and from which direction the arrow came are far from top priority concerns. These preoccupations and questions will kill him if he does not first remove the arrow and deal with the wound. "Dealing" with our wounds appropriately will take us out of the world of philosophical speculation and drop us once again back into the lap of love.

We may be aware that to love our child is terribly risky and that it may in the end lead to tremendous pain, because that child may one day grow to hate us or abandon us, get sick and die or be hurt beyond our control. All the same, we just love them because we must. In an effort to live and be alive in the deepest meaning of what life essentially is, we risk the pain and loss inherent in loving because we must. There is no alternative that makes any reasonable sense. In the same way, loving our self or life or even God is risky business; it may lead to disappointments and pain, but we must love or we will never know what it means to be alive. If we cannot find a way of being alive in this mortal body, we will be led once again to suicide and despair.

Reframing Pain

"Reframing" means to understand things in a new way, to look at them in a different context. The actual content of the picture remains the same, but when we place it in a new frame, it looks different, for better or worse. Michael Jordan missed more shots than almost any other player in professional basketball, but it was not because he was a lousy ballplayer. It was because he was given more chances to throw the ball. Everyone passed him the ball because he was the "go to" guy. That is a different "frame" than if we were to say he missed more than average because he was a poor player, yet the facts about how many shots he actually missed remain the same. The feeling, reaction and response are very different for each "frame of reference." If coaches only saw Jordan in reference to how many shots he missed, they would conclude he is a lousy shot and not have him on the team. In the proper context, the right "frame," Jordan was kept on the team and was paid millions of dollars to keep missing those shots.

Perhaps it is possible to think differently about the shots you have missed. It may be that the events, circumstances and foul-ups that you have experienced do not have the meaning you have assigned them. Perhaps your "missed shots" are the loved ones you have lost, the business ventures that have failed, the people you have hurt. Perhaps some of these failures and losses have been an important part of your development, or it may be that you have won and succeeded in more ways than you now remember. Maybe you have become physically sick so that you could become spiritually well. Perhaps you failed at business so you could excel at poetry. It is quite possible that all your hardships have led you to this place for a reason.

Reframing does not suggest that we should think about anything in a false way, that we should deny any of the facts or pretend that anything is other than what it is. It is a mistake that always makes matters worse. Many times we miss something obvious because of how we are looking at the whole. You have seen those hologram pictures that look like a thousand intersecting lines and colors, but when seen with soft eyes in the right perspective, it suddenly becomes clear that it is a picture of dolphins swimming or the Statue of Liberty.

We might get a flat tire and think the universe is conspiring against us. What if we later discovered that the flat had kept us from being part of a multicar pileup that caused several deaths? Seeing the flat in this frame would not have saved us the trouble and expense of the flat, and we would still have broken down and been inconvenienced, but if we "knew" that it had saved us, we would be free to experience the inconvenience in a different and lighter way.

Some "frames" are built on the facts alone, such as the simple and concrete details of how and why we got the flat: the tire was bald, we drove over a nail and the natural consequence followed. Others' frames are built of faith, such as the belief that the flat came at that particular time for a certain reason. Some can be built around corroborating "evidence," such as the presence of a bad accident up the road that confirms our feeling or suspicion that perhaps the incident served a purpose. Others are never verified one way or another and stand completely on our interpretation. Others' frames may be chosen purposefully because they make the picture more appealing, or in some cases, more dreadful.

We can pick and choose how we will frame things. Although going with things as they are is always best, there are times when we are confronted with absolute uncertainty about how things really are. In such uncertainty, we must choose. We often choose to believe the worst, but perhaps we could just as easily think the best. This is especially true when we are depressed and consistently choose to see everything through a frame of negativity. Others who are paranoid, for instance, see everything through the frame of distrust and suspicion, whether people are against them or not.

Perhaps, as part of our work together, we can play with the frames, look at the world in more than one way and challenge our assumptions just a bit. You might try experimenting with a new approach to understanding your predicament and see what happens. What do you have to lose?

Are You a Butterfly in Process?

Consider the following as an example of framing and reframing.

A butterfly is a caterpillar consumed. Everything the caterpillar once was is sacrificed in the fire of transformation. Its entire life, identity, attachments, skills, beliefs, comforts, orientations and relationships are burnt up in the furnace of some horrible dark cocoon. Everything it previously trusted in or believed is crushed in the crucible of change. However, the cocoon serves as both a suffocating chamber of death and an incubator for a new birth. Metamorphosis is nature's most baffling and grueling process, and her most gracious gift. All this torment and dark loneliness has but one purpose—to bring forth new life.

Although the caterpillar may possibly "know" this meta-morphosis on some level and although it may understand it in some partial way before it occurs, it is nearly impossible to maintain this awareness while it is happening. The pain is too great. The path is too long. A part of this nice little caterpillar may even begin to feel responsible for the pain. It may even entertain guilt. Its condition has forced it to leave behind all its friends and family, it cannot work or perform and there is nothing it can do to improve itself any faster. It may lose sight of the big picture and may forget all about the promise of becoming a butterfly.

While the cocoon is doing its darkest work, the caterpillar must wish at times to return to the way things were. We would not be surprised if it begged to be put out of its misery.

But it can never go back, and death is no solution. So, it patiently endures, and struggles to creep along in the dark toward its unfolding destiny. Something inside, something more than its understanding and will power comes into play and emerges with forces beyond itself, and together this worm and this mystery join to make manifest the miracle of a new life. This transformation, this metamorphosis from worm to wonder is the way of all living things. Barren trees bear fruit, dry stalks shoot forth flowers and the empty sky in time fills with clouds that bring forth the needed rains.

Every living thing longs to be transformed, to grow and change and manifest its original intent, to bring forth its destiny. Acorns become oak trees; apple seeds grow into apple trees. What about humans? Although we are born complete with fingers and toes, heart and head, body and emotion, we are seeded for more— to become a soul, a complete human being in every respect. A cocoon will be necessary. Our creepy, crawly existence among the impermanent and unsatisfactory things of this world is but the initial stage of a life moving toward its purpose and ultimate realization.

Like the caterpillar, we often forget this perspective. We fail to see it, or we do not even believe it is true. This is precisely the equivalent of what happens to us in our darkest times of hopelessness and despair. Disappointment, pain, confusion and loss are there to strip us of our sluglike existence, to free us of our attachments, fears and limitations. Often we resist and want it to all go away. We like our little bug world, and becoming a butterfly is far from our thoughts. We want to be left alone, and we become angry at the cocoon process. At times we just want to die. But we were born to fly, to be transformed from our self-centered, self-indulgent and limited perspective into something more, something resembling God.

This new life comes slowly, gradually, and even after we come into our new form, we remain, like the butterfly, part bug. We will continue to fall and occasionally crawl, but once we have moved through the worst of the initial stages, we will be given wings to "rise above." These "wings" are for us the capacity to let go of all that keeps us down, our willingness to relinquish the past, to forgive, to love and to fly with wings of beauty and creativity.

We may need to be rebirthed a thousand times, but every time we get back up and rise again we take another lesson in flying. Falling, crashing and even "dying" to the life and self we thought we once knew before is no proof that we are destined to remain a caterpillar. It merely verifies the fact that there is something in us that is destined to become more than we once were.

When we feel as if "our life is over," or that "we cannot live like this one more day," our intuition is correct. The life we once had is being phased out, and we must let it go and die to it if we are to be "reborn." We have a larger destiny and purpose. What we are being asked to do is to allow this cocooning, metamorphosis process to work its miracle in us: to hold on, accept the changes, die to the life we once had and allow the larger wisdom of life to initiate us into a new form.

This butterfly analogy is simply another way of framing our experiences of torment, loss and pain. We need not despair or give up if we can imagine this to be true. This may be an initial attempt at faith: to suppose, if ever so tentatively, that there may be an alternate universe, one akin to what Jesus and all the prophets and saints of the ages spoke of, where God is in control and an ultimate good will prevail if we allow it and believe it to be true.

We are born, ideally, to adapt and grow through the experience of pain the way flowers and birds do, but in contrast to the animals and plants of nature, we are also given the capacity to doubt, resist or struggle against what the cocoon of our pain is trying to accomplish in us. This is free will. The task of all true religion is to help realign the human will with the divine will and to remind us of our long forgotten identity and destiny.

By pointing toward the possibility of self-transcendence, forgiveness, love, hope, meaning and joy, all true spirituality attempts to help us move through our pain, to allow us to rise above our pain as well as our unnecessary "suffering" and to heal us of our despair so that we may realize our potential.

CHAPTER 8
Live the Questions

Be patient toward all that is unsolved in your heart and try to love the questions themselves like locked rooms and like books that are written in a very foreign tongue. Do not seek then answers, which cannot be given you because you would not be able to live them. Live the questions now. Perhaps you will then gradually, without noticing it, live along some distant day into the answer.

—R. M. Rilke[1]

We will never be able to answer all our questions. Learning to live with them is key to understanding how to move from desperation to acceptance.

When we face the unbearable and unavoidable, we must approach our pain with a balanced plan of both action and contemplation. We must experience our perplexity fully and without resistance or hesitation. Although we must go through periods of questioning, bargaining, anger, resistance and confusion in order to heal, to move through these experiences we must eventually "live the questions." To live them as they are, unanswered, and sometimes without the possibility of being answered.

Living the questions means living while we still have no answers, living "with" the messiness while maintaining our capacity to love and laugh in full engagement with all that is. We act. We choose. We love. We doubt. We hurt. We wait. In the midst of all this, we remain alive, keeping our hearts open, embracing life and the truth of our being for what it is. Then, and only then, can we begin to live beyond the questions and "perhaps someday," with no guarantees, we "may" come into the answers. Rilke seems to be pointing in the same direction as Christ in saying that the only life worth living is one that is lived in mystery, one that embraces both the action of faith and the contemplation of love, but without any guarantees that all the questions will be answered.

We are given a few "answers," but they never seem absolute in an intellectual sort of way. The "answers" God seems to offer most often are given in the form of reassurances rather than standard solutions. Like a father speaking to his child while going through the House of Horrors at some amusement park, our Father seems to be saying, "It's okay, it's going to be all right," rather than explaining in any detail how all these phantoms and demons are actually made of tin and wire. Life seems to be saying, "I am a gift to you, but I come with a price. I am a complex, variable, incomprehensible mix of joy and pain, and sometimes I am a terrible mess. But you can't live without me. So if you will accept me as I am, I will accept you as you are."

To refuse life's explanation is to refuse life as it is. Many do refuse to accept life on its own terms. This is a fairly common and understandable position to take. A sixty-one-year-old insurance executive recently told me he "refuses to accept defeat in any way." He was resolute and strong willed, acting out of his best "executive suit" mentality, the one he had depended on for many years. He was experiencing significant cognitive slippage, disorientation, confusion and memory impairment, most likely the early stages of dementia. It was terribly sad to watch him as he struggled against his plight, how he fought to maintain his prowess in conversation and how he worked incredibly hard to convince me he was still the man he had always been. Yet he could not find his way to the rest room or identify what day it was. Far sadder than his actual illness was his refusal to accept it.

Paulo Coelho writes, "A warrior accepts defeat. He does not treat it as a matter of indifference, nor does he transform it into a victory. The pain of defeat is bitter to him; he suffers at indifference and becomes desperate with loneliness. After all this has passed, he licks his wounds and begins anew. A warrior knows war is made of many battles; he goes on. Tragedies do happen. We can discover the reason, blame others, imagine how different our lives would be had they not occurred. But none of that is important: they did occur, and so be it. From there onward we must put aside the fear that they awoke in us and begin to rebuild."[2]

This insurance executive could not rebuild his intelligence or his career, but perhaps he could rebuild his love for his wife, slow down his illness through treatment or begin to make peace with his Maker. Not many of us are that courageous. Everything is an unanswered question, unraveling, moving toward extinction, unsatisfactory and dying.

In reconciling these two extremes, we come to rest in the mystery of grace once again. This is the transformative beauty and redemptive miracle of grace. It allows broken things to be okay. This is "good news" for humanity.

Understanding everything is broken is an essential step in healing. It is a truth that cannot be denied, and if we are to make any sense of this life we must take all of it, as it is, into account.

Perhaps "What Appears To Be Broken" Is as It Should Be?

The duality of pitting bad against good, male against female, God against humanity is unfamiliar to many ancient cultures, particularly in the East. It is more common for these cultures to speak of the integration of opposing values: of black and white, the yin and the yang. Interestingly, the most advanced mystics in the Jewish and Christian traditions also echo this sentiment. Living the questions becomes a more familiar and even appropriate approach given this understanding.

Christian mystics who understand that these apparently oppositional qualities are in fact an integral part of the whole as it must be say that things are broken by design and cannot ever be otherwise because they are meant to stay this way. No amount of tinkering or wishing can make things unbroken or unbreakable. Instead of trying to fix everything, they say we should learn to improve on what can be improved and accept what cannot be improved without insisting that things be other than they are. If we fail in this, our only recourse is despair, and when despair wins the day, suicide can only be a few short steps away.

Trying to fix everything is normal. We all do it and are all frustrated by our efforts every day. Once we get our health in good shape, the finances go down the drain . We get the finances under control and the kids start acting up. Things finally settle down, then about that time we have to deal with the death of our father. He passes away and we survive it only to face our own failing health. The new car gets a scratch on it, the vacation is ruined by rain and a friend is offended by a thoughtless remark.

This frustration and the realization that we can never seem to get everything right and make it stay that way can be depressing. However, reality is not meant to depress us. It is speaking to us, as the truth of things is apt to do regardless how it comes, and it is trying to teach us we are not in control of everything, that nothing will ever be perfect and that the "answer" does not lie in our eventually figuring it all out and fixing it.

We are being asked to live with brokenness, to learn from it and to appreciate it just as it is. Everything includes our self, others, the world and God. It includes suffering and imperfection and brokenness in all its manifestations.

Created things are broken through no fault of our own. They are healed only by our proper use of the powers we are given. Through love and acceptance we can touch this crippled world with our compassion by refusing to get stuck in our anger or arrogance. By touching this brokenness with our gentleness and care, we become part of the "solution" without insisting that the world be paradise. We can make this imperfect world more perfect by making it a world full of crippled people who are treated with respect, acceptance and care, a world where able-bodied individuals open doors for the lame.

It is hard enough to deal with the brokenness that is not our fault, but it is more difficult when we are the ones responsible for the damage. Yet, even when we are the ones who have broken things, we are still challenged to touch the broken places with healing love, acceptance and forgiveness rather than to tear things apart more by anger and rejection.

When we break a relationship by being ignorant, self-centered and cruel, we can heal it, not by trying to make it perfect next time or by punishing ourselves, but by owning up to our faults, asking forgiveness and attempting to be more authentic and loving next time out. When we have broken all our chances to make something of our lives, when we have broken our health and self-respect through repeated addictions and failures, when we have broken our promises to God, we can still bring healing to these torn and fractured places. More than ever, we are called to accept the brokenness and to heal it through our love for ourselves.

Anyone who is willing to heal personal brokenness with self-understanding and forgiveness is incapable of suicide. All of this can only be accomplished through grace, by an encounter with and participation in that which "holds up" all this brokenness.

In Psalm 107 we see four interesting "types" or groups of suffering individuals. The first group "wandered in desert wastes, finding no way to an inhabited town; hungry and thirsty, their soul fainted within them." This may represent the land of the "hungry ghosts," of addiction and attachment, where we are lost from our true home in a wasteland of need that can never be fulfilled. The second group are those who "sat in darkness and in gloom, prisoners in misery and irons," with their "hearts bowed down with hard labor." These are the ones who experience life as a constant struggle, the group Jesus referred to as those who "labor and are heavy laden." This particular type suffering may relate to the times when we rely exclusively on our own strength and experience the exhaustion and imprisonment of an ego-centered existence.

The third group is described as those "who were sick through their sinful ways, and because of their iniquities suffered affliction." I imagine we have all felt the pain of our own "iniquity," when our poor choices, stubbornness, meanness, mistreatment of others or pride has turned upon us and afflicted us. We have added to the difficulties inherent in the human condition by ignoring wise counsel and chasing illusions. Lastly, we see the group that "went down to the sea in ships, doing business on the mighty waters." But God "commanded and raised the stormy wind, which lifted up the waves of the sea." These poor souls were tossed "up to heaven" and "down to the depths" and "their courage melted" as they "reeled and staggered like drunkards." They were "at wits end." It seems to me this group represents the suffering we all experience as we find ourselves reeling from the immensity and confusion of life's ever-changing, unpredictable and tempestuous seas. We may lose courage and approach wits end or stagger about like a drunkard if in the midst of this we lose our centeredness in God.

The most interesting thing about these four types of suffering is that in every case, the Psalmist follows his description with this phrase; "they cried to the LORD in their trouble, he saved them from their distress." Sometimes he "healed and delivered them from destruction," and other times he "satisfied their thirst." He "brought them out of darkness," "made the storm be still" and turned "a parched land into springs of water." In all of this falling, destruction, despair and doubt, whether the troubles were initiated by God or by the rebellion of the people, God always reacted and responded by "saving them from their distress." There never was and never will be a time when a person in distress cries out to the Lord and is left abandoned.[3]

When Idols Break

Our ideals and ideas, our sense of self, the things we attach the most importance to can become like little idols. Little idols can become like false gods, but these gods fail us, and when they do we fall into despair. Anthony Bloom writes, "In a way despair is at the center of things....We must be prepared for a period when God is not there for us and we must be aware of not trying to substitute a false god."[4] When God does not seem to be there for us and our idols break apart, we must be careful not to replace them with other equally false or misleading attachments or notions.

Idols are little gods we have invented out of the stuff of ordinary life. They are the things and people and ideas that we have come to believe have the power to save us. Like a primitive bushman who finds a transistor radio and believes there are hundreds of little people inside there talking and singing, we in our ignorance have picked up certain promising and novel items in our immediate world and projected a whole host of unrealistic expectations onto them. These "items" become our idols.

If a snort of cocaine makes me suddenly feel euphoric and more alive than anything ever has, I may come to believe it contains the answer to my life. When one girl makes me finally feel worthy and loved, it is easy for me to believe she is the only hope in the world I have of ever being whole and to conclude that I cannot live without her. These things and events quickly become gods to us. We would never call them that, but they assume the position in our psyche of a god. We begin to live for this god, we believe in this god and we depend on it for our survival.

Taking the position of gods in our hearts and minds, these are the things to which we attach the most importance: the beliefs, objects and feelings for which we live and upon which we depend. We all make security, pleasure, self-reliance, notoriety, beauty and perfection our "gods" at one time or another. We come to rely on these things and to give them our full attention and faith. Unconsciously, we believe in them and expect them to save us, to be there for us in times of trouble and to provide us with the security and happiness we deserve—but they fall apart. Sooner or later the drug wears off, truth breaks through the illusions we hold dear and we are left with the shell of a broken god.

When Beliefs about God Replace His Reality

Our ideas and images about God are constantly being broken because even the one true God can be made out to be one of our little idols. When we give God characteristics that are inconsistent with his reality, we make our idea of God a sort of idol fashioned after our own ideas about "God."

It is natural to project onto "God" our infantile wishes, ego-centered ideas and limited conceptualizations, but by doing so we reduce him to less than he truly is. This reduced version of "God" can unwittingly become a small breakable image that we adhere to in place of the one true God who is beyond images and concepts. The only appropriate approach to the idea of God is to maintain an open heart filled with wonder and awe, expectant of love but not easily enchanted by rigid concepts. As St. Gregory of Nyssa put it, "Concepts create idols; only wonder comprehends anything."[5]

This is what Meister Eckhart meant when he said, "...the ultimate and highest leave-taking is leaving God for God."[6] Many have already left the "God" you once thought you knew. Now the task is to replace this breakable image of God with a different perception.

For example, we commonly envision God as the good provider in the sky who meets all our needs. This idea contains the truth, but our idea of that truth is twisted to mean that God will meet all our needs according to our plan rather than his. When we are struck down with illness and do not recover, our God appears to be stumbling and falling down on the job. Rather than ridding our self of God because we perceive him as failing us, we are being called to die to our false image of God so that we may be united to the one true God.

The deconstruction of everything we thought we ever knew about God is a prerequisite to discovering God on his own terms. This is important for the person who may be recovering from a lost faith. No one who has found religion to be shallow, controlling and demeaning can be expected to return to it. Religion as we know it must often be left behind. What is needed in this instance is a deconstruction of all our previous versions of God and religion in order to discover the heart of God for ourselves.

Every false image, misguided expectation, poorly placed dependence and inaccurate belief will eventually fail us. When gods break, we will be forced to find the God that does not break. The alternative is to follow our broken gods down into the abyss of despair and possibly suicide.

"The courage to be," writes theologian Paul Tillich, "is rooted in the god who appears when god disappears in the anxiety of doubt."[7] Anyone who finds the "courage to be" through the disappearance of the false god and the appearance of the True One is incapable of suicide.

It is certainly possible for the embattled, discouraged and suicidal person to embrace or develop greater amounts of love, hope, faith and wisdom in order to transform what was once a path of self-destruction into a path of self transcendence.

There is never a better opportunity for spiritual renewal than in times of crisis. The greater the crisis, the greater the opportunity. Being near the brink of suicide is a perfect example. At no other point in a person's life does one need more desperately to be forgiven, accepted, understood, healed and enlightened as when they are on the verge of giving up. "Good news" could not come at a better time.

The foundation and source of all such "good news," and of every spiritual gift, is grace. Grace is by definition the unmerited, undeserved and freely given favor, redemption, forgiveness and healing that flows directly from the Source of all universal love to the least deserving mortal. The absolute beauty of grace is that one cannot work for it or earn it. We are not required to believe any particular doctrine, practice any good works, join any religious movement or cover up any of our past mistakes. All we have to do is be open, broken, receptive and willing to receive grace and heal. The healing is gradual but absolute. It is freely given but never forcefully imposed. It is always available and requires only our cooperation. *Cooperation* means nothing more than to have a broken, contrite spirit and a willingness to heal. This willingness and openness gives grace a place to plant the seeds of love, wisdom, faith and hope.

Right now, if you are at your lowest, you are already broken. You are halfway there. Everything leads back to God. Just as gold is purified and forced into becoming its true essential nature by being repeatedly exposed to the fire of annihilation, so we too are refined in the furnace. We do not need to make any efforts whatsoever to expose ourselves to this "annihilation," for it will come to us uninvited over and again.

If we are not inclined to see things this way, we are left to face our suffering without meaning. Viktor Frankl defines despair as "suffering without meaning."[8] To endure the repeated insults of life without meaning is to invite, or even guarantee, despair.

The Gifts of Loss

How would our life be different if we were certain that every unwanted difficulty had a long-range purpose and that each and every uninvited bit of suffering had some meaning? For example, suppose your daughter needed a kidney transplant and you qualified as her donor. Your suffering and sacrifice would certainly be meaningful in such a case.

Merton says that no one is ever called to "suffer merely for the sake of suffering," but that we are called to "make it holy" by faith and by understanding, and that "the things that wreck our outer being only perfect us within."[9] He elaborates: "The trials that seem to defy our hope and ruin the very foundations of all patience are meant, by the Spirit of God, to make our hope more and more perfect, basing it entirely in God, removing every visible support that can be found in this world."[10]

Such explanations of suffering are common not only in Christianity but in nearly every religion. Sacrifice leads to bliss, death precedes resurrection and from out of destruction and chaos comes the creation of all good things.

These are universally common beliefs and form the bases of many spiritual practices, not the least of which is one referred to as the practice of "transforming difficulties into the path," a common concept in Buddhist practice. "This involves consciously taking our unwanted sufferings, the sorrows of our life, the struggles within us and the world outside, and using them as a ground for the nourishment of our patience and compassion, the place to develop greater freedom," advises Jack Kornfield.[11]

Suffering can have a purpose and make sense if we use it and allow it to do its perfect work. The New Testament author James advises, "My brothers and sisters, whenever you face trials of any kind, consider it nothing but joy, because you know that the testing of your faith produces endurance; and let endurance have its full effect, so that you may be mature and complete, lacking in nothing."[12] "Lacking in nothing" is a big promise.

If you knew that all the unwanted, uncontrollable and incomprehensible aspects in your life, the sickness and poverty and betrayal, was actually life's way of helping you rather than harming you, would you then take a different approach to suffering? If you were certain, for instance, that you had been unjustly imprisoned because God intended for you to become free of all worldly obligations long enough for him to fill you with the spirit of his power and love, would you then be able to tolerate the injustice differently?

If we had such a belief, or better yet, if we knew for certain that all suffering was intended for our benefit, would we find hope in place of despair, renewal in place of retreat and acceptance in the arms of a loving Father where we had once experienced an impersonal chaotic universe?

In place of resistance, anger and turmoil, might we experience equanimity, peace and gratitude if this little idea were more than an ideal, but an absolute truism?

CHAPTER 9
Soul Recovery: The Secret Center of the World

When, with you asleep, I plunge into your soul, and I listen, with my ear on your naked breast, to your tranquil heart, it seems to me that, in its deep throbbing, I surprise the secret center of the world.

—Juan Ramon Jimenez[1]

Soul is the poetry and passion of life. It is the lucid fire burning at the center of our being. Soul is the nesting place of all longing and the cradle of unspeakable joy and unbearable pain. It contains the whisper of love's innocence and the echo of infinity. Soul is the still point around which human activities, concerns, attachments and aversions spin. It is the vacant heart of darkness as well as the vibrant void through which the living waters rise up and refresh the tired and weary. Soul is the empty fullness that blinks on and off at the base of our existence.

A healthy soul radiates wellness in the midst of life's imperfections, allowing meaning and vitality to appear in the presence of death and decay. Soul makes one full the way nature fulfills itself, not in the absence of death and winter and darkness, but through the careful integration of these elements with their opposites. Soul strives to incorporate the whole world of pain and pleasure into a cohesive unit, blending despair with hope, personal power with effortless grace, fantasy with reality, solitude with the need for others.

Lacking soul health, one is apt to become overwhelmed with life's paradoxes, demands and uncertainties. The soul-shallow individual is likely to be sickly, easily discouraged, dispirited, disintegrated and disturbed. The soul's condition will determine one's maturity, optimism, realism, integrity and, in the end, one's quality of life. Weakness of soul leaves one vulnerable in a world of apparent disorder and meaningless chaos.

Soul never promises perfection or an easy life. It offers the hope of endurance and even enjoyment of a life lived by an imperfect person in the midst of an irregular and incomplete world. We are all dependent on soul. Will power and intellect alone are insufficient. Belief in some external intervention without the willingness to participate in our recovery falls flat, while soul virtue and soul maturity call forth one's participation in the miracle of the universe's willingness to help and sustain one through the ambiguities and murkiness of human life.

Soul is active as well, engaging and alive, waiting for our return and calling us out, then responding to our movement. Robert Bly writes, "If you give a hair to the soul it will cover the hair with gold. If you make a road toward it, it will respond and cut down brush to make a road toward you."[2] Soul wants you, and will reward your efforts to find your way home.

Through soul, the "supernatural" becomes a naturally flowing integrated part of the whole rather than some contrived or artificial flash of momentary insight or deliverance. God is such a central player in the soulful life that coincidence, luck, happenstance and fortunate events are simply accepted as love notes from the divine. Unfortunate accidents and unforeseen difficulties are also accepted equally as from the hand of God. Everything relates back to the meaning of the relationship to the divine because this relationship is no longer alien or forced, but the soul's natural environment.

Through love, soul illuminates and sanctifies the mundane particulars, allowing order and meaning to shine through the chaos and apparent insignificance of the concrete routines of our all too human lives. By not allowing us to overly spiritualize the secular, wringing it dry of its complexity, and by refusing to reduce the divine to no more than a pantheistic expression of a faceless God, soul allows us to be as we are while initiating us in between both worlds. Soul knows all too well that these two worlds are not in opposition or altogether different from each other.

Like a "Jesus factor," soul gives meaning to a life of weeping and laughter, toil and peace, solitude and community, crucifixion and resurrection. Without insisting on pleasure without pain or accomplishment without failure, soul makes life "as it is" bearable.

Most of our natural lives are marked by the wish or illusion of eventual perfection or complete satisfaction. When we find that impossible, we are tempted to abandon ourselves to hedonistic pleasures or to sink into despair and despondency. It is the rare person who can accept the imperfections, challenges, losses and disappointments in herself and the world and still love herself, others and all of life just as it is. Such an individual is truly a person of soul.

Although "soul" may sound like some hip phrase from the '70s or some odd metaphysical term, it is in fact a simple and basic concept. In music, we might say elevator "Muzak" is a familiar tune with the soul removed. In painting, we might say a paint-by-number picture is art without "soul." In life, some might say a heroin-addicted prostitute has "lost her soul."

On the positive side, we have all heard a "very soulful" rendition of "America the Beautiful" or witnessed the power of a "great soul" such as Gandhi or Walt Whitman. Soul is that quality within a person, place or thing that transforms it into pure poetry.

Soul can never be completely understood, interpreted or defined. Like the experience of love, the same applies to soul. We can rely on love and soul and can speak about them without having to prove or define them. As we become more soulful, we become more comfortable with the idea that "soul" involves all that defies definition and control: the sacred, beautiful and creative grace that dignifies the spaces of our sorrow and joy. To live only among the profane, ugly, mechanistic and transient whims of a meaningless life is to lack soul.

No one is actually without soul. Some, however, are more skilled or gifted in nurturing and manifesting soul than others. The quality of soul appears to be partly determined by a combination of skillful attention mixed with gift and grace, but in any case it is clear there are differences in the fullness, quality or intensity of soul from one person to the next.

Some seem to take no pleasure in soul at all. For these people, the value of any person, place or thing is determined by its power, calculable worth, immediate satisfaction, tangible benefit or time-space currency. Soul speaks another language. Its "benefits" are as subtle as the love of a parent or a treasured moment, and to those who understand the value of these things and the language of soul, there is nothing more important than soul.

The value of soul is in the here and now. Soul is not about the life hereafter or divine interventions and miracles, although it may effect or open the way to some of these things. Soul is about living here in the real world, right now. The spirituality of soul is plain, common and real. It can teach us how to live the uneventful and mundane moments with poetic vision, transparent integrity, genuine care and an honest appreciation for what is. Soul is fueled by an unseen inspiration and transcendent sensibility that prizes wisdom above information, mercy above judgment and life over death. Washing the dishes is still washing the dishes, but to the soulful individual there is meaning in the suds.

The Soul's Gifts

Mostly, the soul's job is to sustain and enrich life. One of its prime functions is to keep us alive and hopeful in the midst of all the sad madness inherent in this world. If our soul loses its grit in tough times, we will be overcome. Soul empowers one to continually wonder, hope and struggle without caving in or giving up. When soul is weak and sick we see its symptoms manifest as an irrational mind, a pessimistic attitude, a bitter competitiveness, a mean-spirited constitution and a foul mood. There may also be paranoia, jealousy, hatred—every sort of unpleasantness. This does not mean that a soul-invigorated person is without dispirited or loathsome moments or that there are not reasons for unpleasantness other than the condition of one's soul. But if the soul is well, it is of secondary importance what happens around us.

The terminally ill person requires serious intervention; hospitalizations, antibiotics, surgeries, blood transfusions, maybe even vital organ replacements. A little bed rest is not enough. So the suicidal person with a lethally ill soul may need radical surgery at first, including, but not limited to, reorganizing their entire life, cutting off all contacts with other infectious individuals, renouncing all previous attachments and replacing their old heart with a new one. This takes a willingness to trust the surgeon, be put to sleep, go under the knife and pay the big bill. In other words, it is no small matter to restore the sick soul to health. Although the payoff is significant, it may cost us initially. Soul restoration not only involves rebirth of the new but the death and burial of the old.

Once reborn, the soul needs to be maintained. It requires attention and care. There are hundreds of saints and spiritual writers one can consult on how to provide this ongoing care and maintenance.

The soul, according to Thomas Moore, is "a piece of the sky and a chunk of the earth lodged in the heart of every human being."[3]

Here is the challenge. Sky needs sky food and needs to play among the clouds. The chunk of earth needs to be dirty and grounded. What this means is that in order to be soul-full human beings we must learn to balance sky with earth. Too much or too little of either will throw us off balance, and the absence of either will collapse us in the direction of our lack.

The health of one's soul is determined by balancing an appropriate level of activity and an equally appropriate level of receptivity, part human will and part diving grace. "The paradox here is that you will always have a test to invoke grace [or soul], and you need grace to pass the test. You can't just suddenly become courageous; you have to act out courage to know you have courage."[4] This comment appears in Caroline Myss's book *Sacred Contracts,* where she discusses the characters in the *Wizard of Oz.* Myss observes that the scarecrow, the tin man, the lion and Dorothy were all called to bring forth their gifts first in order to see that they were indeed gifted with them already. So it is with soul.

Certain characteristics of one's soul may be predetermined, as James Hillman emphasizes in his book, *The Soul's Code.* He says that each one of us is "coded" in a sense, fated from birth to have a certain degree of potential or a particular set of qualities that distinguish our soul and give it a unique set of callings and gifts. Some are "born" to be artists, leaders, visionaries and such. His theory is that we are free to develop this potentiality or ignore it, and that whenever one's "code" is denied, one's entire life is unfulfilled and frustrated.[5]

This is what Christian mystics refer to as our calling and spiritual gifts. They too say we will remain desperately unhappy until we find and follow our inner calling and develop and share our gifts. Doing so is a critical aspect of one's soul. We have all had dreams and aspirations of what our lives could be. Like Jonathan Livingston Seagull, we have all at one time seen more for our lives than fighting for scraps among the common crowd of uninspired earthbound bottom-feeder birds. We have caught a brief glimpse of that star within us, and we yearn to let it shine. It is so easy to lose sight of this, to give in to the habitual, copy-cat, humdrum world of eating and sleeping and trying to survive with no sign of poetry in sight.

These apparently "encoded" gifts as well as those chosen and developed by a person's will and inclination are both equally fragile and depend on one's cooperation and involvement. Those gifted with great souls like Gandhi and Martin Luther King were just as free to become dishonest car salesmen or junkies. Although it is impossible for me to "will" myself into becoming another Rumi, I can certainly choose whether or not I will write spiritual poetry or shut it down.

Just as fate and personal willingness each play a role in the development of soul, so does adversity and our response to it. Just as gold is refined of its impurities by fire and an irritating grain of sand in the oyster's soft insides becomes a pearl, so one's soul develops through and by the stress and fire of everyday disappointments and irritants. Soul is given and gifted by divine order, but it is equally developed and defined by human choice.

Emotional experiences may serve as an example. On one level, emotions are simply electrical and impersonal impulses crossing neuronal pathways and producing sensations in the organism. These things we call anger, joy or sadness. Neurosurgeons can manually stimulate specific locations in the brain tissue and produce feelings of fear, anger, sexual excitement, sadness or happiness. These feelings originate in the gray matter of brain tissue and can be manipulated, yet they are equally mysterious and without physical location.

Where is mind? What is feeling? Where does the experience of meaning or love come from? Where do awareness and faith originate, and how do they differ from electrical impulses running through our nerve endings? How is it that the physical brain can experience a self, consciousness, goodness, humor, surprise, creativity, hope and beauty? Just as "mind" is the metaphysical ghost that transforms brain tissue and cells into something more than matter, so "soul" is what transforms the heart from a beating mound of flesh and blood into a quivering, magical center of divinely charged inspiration.

All this can be endlessly debated, of course, and I am not suggesting that I can define soul or offer a definitive theory about the origin or development of soul. All I am trying to point out is that there is an important inner seed of soul destiny and star wonder within us that we can either trample until we have no reason to live, or nurture and protect until it enlightens our darkened world.

Soul Logic

In some respects, this may all sound a bit strange. Soul logic differs from purely intellectual reason. At times the soul has reasons the mind cannot comprehend. Working in and through soul is different than most kinds of problem solving or healing. We typically look at what is "wrong" and try to fix it or make it go away. In medicine we set the broken bone. In auto mechanics we replace the worn-out starter with a new one. With soul work, change occurs slowly within a mystery, nurtured by silence, echoing with a love that is incomprehensible. The key to such soul healing always lies within or near the symptom.

The soul speaks to us in parables, riddles and sometimes myth. Every fascination has an element of dread. Every dark pull has within itself an element of light. Hidden within the obvious is its counterpart. At the core of the suicidal preoccupation is actually the desire for life. We do not become suicidal, for instance, unless we have first longed for or tasted life's fullness and promise and been shut down. If we never cared, we would not have known the bitterness of loss and lack.

In soul work we cannot simply reject the wish to die. We must listen to it. By exploring it fully and seeing within it the opposite by remembering our previously hopeful and joyful hearts, we can begin to appreciate what needs to be done. We cannot simply force suicidal thoughts out of our head without also recultivating our wish to live. Once this meaning or reason to live is recovered and our hearts are softened once again, suicidal thoughts will spontaneously drop from sight.

To recover the soul's capacity to live is an art. As in any artistic work, one's subconscious, spontaneous, flexible, creative and passive capabilities are more important than one's directive, controlling or willful ones. In fact, too much consciously directed and determined effort often hinders one's progress.

As in psychotherapy, the one who is most desperately set on finding the "twelve secret steps to happiness" is the one who is the least likely to be able to go with the unfolding flow of the relationship and process of change that leads to the deepest levels of healing. Thomas Moore again notes, "Care of the soul observes the paradox whereby the muscled, strong-willed pursuit of change can actually stand in the way of substantive transformation."[6]

Antoine De St.-Exupery suggested, "If you want to build a ship, don't drum up the men to gather wood, divide the work and give orders. Instead, teach them to yearn for the vast and endless sea."[7] The key to "building" a soul that holds the promise of tomorrow is to cultivate a rich and passionate desire for the vast and endless sea of love, peace, joy and God's dear presence.

Forget about working so hard. The work will get done once you get the vision and the passion.

In a similar vein, Moore again notes, "…in the care of the soul, there is trust that nature heals, that much can be accomplished by non-doing."[8] Non-doing is invoked by all mystical traditions as one of the secret keys to unlocking the spiritual potential. True soul virtue is powered by grace, and it is through love that we discover love. It is through God's Spirit that we find God's presence. It is in being willing to let go and trust, to "allow" God to arise in us that makes the journey possible.

Soul is a worker of paradox and surprise. In the midst of imperfection, soul asserts that imperfection is the norm for all humanity. Soul tells us that imperfection must be acknowledged and accepted, while a "perfection" of sorts also already exists in things as they are. It is always "both/and" with soul, never "either/or." We find perfection in the imperfections; we realize our self in the all and the all in our self, always finding the brightest gem of radiance in the dullness.

Moments of pain and worthlessness contain the seed of healing and great meaning. Soul is in constant flux, growing and expanding, contracting and shriveling, crying out for attention one moment and bearing gifts of illumination the next. Similar to art, it is a greatly undervalued and misunderstood repository of one's unrealized potential, unexamined conflicts and veiled identity.

Soul straddles the regions between body and spirit, self and other, imminence and transcendence, attempting to integrate all opposing energies, internal and external, as well as the past, present and future.

Like a lover in waiting, soul longs for the caresses and care of the person who is too much engaged in the business and battles of daily life. Soul is never lost. It is merely neglected, frightened, abandoned and denied at times. It is threatened, so it hides. Its voice is muffled. Its nature is naturally strong but sensitive.

Soul is a gentleman, subtly alluring the human animal into its secret garden without forcing its own agenda. Soul longs to inspire travels, joys, relationships, parenting. It wants to accompany and empower us through the celebrations and challenges of human life, but it will not demand to be known or heard.

Clearing the Way

Soul needs only a little encouragement, some clearing out of the things that scare it and a comfortable place to unfold.

In order to heal and expand soul, we have to rid it of any obvious poisons, wounds or malfunctioning parts. A few of the primary killers of soul healing and growth are doubt, ignorance, resentment, lethargy, self-rejection and attachment to failure. Can you step out in faith, begin with sufficient wisdom, forgive the past, find the energy and enthusiasm to do the work, and believe that you can and deserve to receive fullness of life?

First of all, to be rid of doubt, we need faith. To have faith, we need to step out in faith. This is again a paradox. We cannot wait until we are certain that we "feel" enough faith or know it will work. We just begin to trust. Trusting must be based on a realistic appraisal of what God can and will do. We can start with an openhanded trust, saying, "God, I trust you to show me what you want me to see, to move whatever obstacles you care to move and leave the rest; I will accept your decision." This will keep us from being foolish or disappointed and will open the way for us to enter into an acceptance of God's will.

Secondly, dispelling ignorance is done in a similar way. We do not have to "understand" everything in order to be wise. Being wise enough to overcome the ignorance that keeps soul in a dark and confusing place is to begin by recognizing that we will never be intelligent enough to figure everything out. In essence, we can begin by acknowledging our ignorance and by looking at things the way they are rather than how we wish them to be. Wisdom begins by recognizing the truth of our limitations.

In order to be free of ignorance and doubt we must also take a step toward forgiveness. We must forgive God, our self and everyone we hold anything against. Lethargy can be overcome simply by making small beginning movements in the right direction. There was a man in the New Testament who said he wanted to believe but needed help with his unbelief. That was enough for Jesus. We don't say, here I am Lord, ready to walk the life of a saint, any more than we can show up at the piano teacher's house and say, here I am ready to practice eighteen hours a day and perform at Carnegie Hall. We need only ask to be shown the first and most fundamental notes, and then practice those a few minutes every day. With persistence and the belief that our steps will pay off, we will grow eventually to manifest all that grace is capable of producing in us.

All of these movements—to find faith, wisdom, release of our bitterness, energy to persist and the willingness to receive—are dependent on the love of God. The love of God is revealed to those who believe in it, accept the absolute necessity of it, refuse to live without it, acknowledge the incomprehensible nature of its appearance and persist in finding the grace needed to make it manifest.

"God opposes the proud, but gives grace to the humble," says James.[9] Grace is given, not earned. "Draw near to God and he will draw near to you."[10] He comes to us as we move toward him. Clearing the soul of its obstructions starts here.

There is a path to God that is right for you. When you are open and ready, you will find it.

CHAPTER 10
Loving Yourself

The way to recover the soul must begin with self-love. If we cannot make peace with ourselves, if we find it impossible to forgive ourself and if we will not allow ourselves the chance to be happy, we never will be. We are our own worst enemy. When we are against ourself, we will find a way to make certain we remain miserable. If we do not think we deserve another chance, we will block ourselves from it. If we despise ourselves, we will undermine our opportunities to excel. Nothing will help us as long as we are determined to hurt ourselves.

Angela wants to jump off a bridge onto the path of an oncoming truck. She says she "lacks the courage" of her brother, who hung himself in their basement. She found him hanging there lifeless and blue. Now she wants to do the same but says she "doesn't have the guts." I say, "It doesn't take guts to kill yourself; it takes guts to live." However, she is not accepting it because she hates herself.

She has never loved herself because she has never been properly loved. Her father left her when she was an infant. Her mother told her she wished she had never been born. As a biracial child, white kids rejected her for being black, and black kids hated her for being white. Lovers and friends rejected her along the way, and now she has given up on herself and has made the rejection of others her own position against herself. She has turned hatred of herself into a way of life, a mode of being.

It is very difficult to help her because she sees herself as unworthy to be helped. She is unlovable, ugly, unwanted, repulsive and vile in her own estimation. Attempts to build her self-esteem are rebuffed. She is determined to stay mad at herself. Although my heart breaks for her and I know God's heart breaks a thousand times more, there is barely a place in her for love to enter. Without self-love she will not allow herself to be loved by another. Her wish to be dead is partially due to social learning, poor parenting and traumatic events of the past, but it is sustained in the present by a persistent unwillingness to see herself as lovable and worthy to live. This intolerance, impatience, lack of consideration, judgmental attitude and unforgivingness toward herself is the rot in her soul, which, if uncorrected, may well lead to her self-inflicted death.

She will have to love herself first before anything else can have a chance to work. As long as she continues to hate herself, she will refuse to take medications, undermine her positive attributes, dismiss all positive feedback and continue to think of ways to harm herself. With the least bit of self-concern she could give herself the opportunity to be well, but without that, no amount of intervention will stop her self-destructive ways.

Don is a forty-four-year-old professional who was forced to begin dialysis nine months ago. His wife says everything has changed since then. He used to be a regular family man, but now he is bitter and distant. He refuses his medical care and goes on frantic cocaine binges, disappearing for days at a time. Recently he was gone for four days and left a suicide note before trying to kill himself with an overdose of drugs and pills. He was unconscious and very near death when he got to the hospital.

He lived. When he regained consciousness he tried to run out of the intensive care unit to finish the job. I had to detain him by a court order. He was upset with me and thought that God was unfair, but I thought God *was* fair with him since he lived through this near-death attempt. I thought about how fortunate he was to have a loving wife and kids who still wanted him and needed him. His wife talked about how healthy and different he was before, and how involved with the kids and full of life he was prior to his illness. In my mind I could picture him before all this, cutting his grass at home, enjoying a barbeque with the kids and finding pleasure in building a home for his family. I could see it all back in place with the proper treatment.

In wondering what treatment would work best, I knew a forced detainment was needed, but it was also clear that the root of his condition would never change until he was willing to love himself in all of his weakness. I thought of how critical it was for him now to accept himself as a person who had a medical condition, one who was no longer invincible and tough, but needy, sick and weak. It seemed so clear that the root of his suicidal self-rejection was based on this bitter and prejudicial attitude he held toward that which was weak and broken in him. Nothing could "fix" this until he could learn to love himself as he was now.

One final example: a thirty-six-year-old mother of two was rushed into the emergency department at three a.m. She was covered in blood as a result of slashing both her wrists. This attractive and healthy woman was in frenzied torment—fighting, screaming obscenities, spitting at the nurses and spattering blood everywhere. This was a painful sight to see. I held my hand on her ankle and tried to calm her as the nurses were screaming back at her and struggling to keep her still.

The emergency department physician was stitching her up and she was far too agitated to talk, so I slipped out back to an empty hall and wept. She was the third suicidal person I had seen that night. All the suffering of humanity seemed to hang around my neck like a string of dead corpses. I sobbed the way men do, leaning silently against the wall, stoic and aloof. I was too professional, too masculine to sob like a little child. My insides were torn apart by all the hatred and cruelty that this wounded world pours upon itself. In that moment, I again had the revelation that clearly self-hatred is the devil's most effective tool.

Self-Rejection Is the Only Thing That Hinders God's Love

I have wondered where God is in all this madness. Self-hatred is frequently the final and insoluble obstruction to the flow of all the healing and help that is possible. So many are unable and unwilling to let themselves be touched, changed and made whole once again.

The infinite mercy of God can barely break through to those who despise themselves and are unwilling to be helped, forgiven and loved. To change this understanding and become open to the love of God we must begin with humility. Refusing to accept ourselves is masked hostility, not humility. To actually see our true unworthiness and inability to make ourselves acceptable to God is the beginning of humility, and this sets the stage for grace. This is a central part of the Christ story: that we can never be good enough on our own. Rather than making this insufficiency in ourselves a reason to hate and reject ourselves, in Christ it now means we have reason to rejoice because we are accepted by God just as we are. This acceptability before God through Christ is the beginning of self-acceptance for even the most notorious self-haters of all. If God accepts you as you are, and he does, then you must learn to like yourself as you are as well.

This is a big step for some. You may be thinking that if you love yourself now as you are, you may never change. Yet, the opposite is true. It is only after we learn to accept ourselves just as we are that we discover the power to change. Grace gives us the power to change because in grace we are initiated into the flame of living love, and love makes all things possible.

We may have lived horrible worthless lives. We may have wounded those we love, robbed and cheated and distorted every good thing we have ever known. We have failed because we are human. We may have acted out our ugliness because we have been hurt and are angry. We have been uninformed, ignorant and blind. We were born imperfect. We have been immature in some ways. It has not been completely our fault, although we certainly have played our part. For that we are sorry. For the part we had little control of, we accept without blaming ourselves or anyone else. We want a new start, and we take the first step by acknowledging our mistakes and accepting the realties of who we have become to this point. Then we pray to improve, to become better people, to take full responsibility for what we have done, knowing change will not happen all at once. We start with being sick, then apply a little grace toward ourselves, and then trust God to lead us onward from there.

"The first step toward finding God, Who is Truth, is to discover the truth about myself: and if I have been in error, the first step to truth is the discovery of my error," is how Thomas Merton put it.[1]

The most hopeful and important thing about grace is that it allows for, invites and, in fact, requires its participants to come as they are. There are no requirements other than a sincere and willing heart. Bruce Springsteen has a wonderful song entitled "The Land of Hope and Dreams," where, in contrast to the old song about the train that "don't carry no gamblers," this train, the train of hope and dreams, the soul train of God's overwhelming love, carries whores, addicts, losers, lost souls, misguided fools and every sort of mangled and marginalized misanthrope the planet has to offer.[2]

It is our imperfections that God wants. Grace is looking for sinners, losers, whores, drunks, lost souls of every kind. None of us can offer clean hands and clean hearts to God. We are invited to bring our troubled, misspent, foolish, unremarkable and broken selves to the altar of life and to trust the sweetness of grace to sanctify our incompleteness. Merton again writes, "As long as we are on earth, our vocation is precisely to be imperfect, incomplete, insufficient in ourselves, changing, hapless, destitute and weak, hastening toward the grave."[3]

St. Thérèse of Lisieux expressed this beautifully in her autobiography. At a point late in her journey, when she had already accomplished much in the way of spiritual perfection, she writes, "In the days to come it may be that my present state will seem most imperfect, but I am no longer surprised at anything and I feel no distress at seeing my complete helplessness. On the contrary, I glory in it and every day I expect to discover fresh flaws in myself. In fact, this revelation of my nothingness does me much more good than being enlightened on matters of faith."[4]

The fourteenth-century mystic and scholar Meister Eckhart put it this way, "To get at the heart of God in his greatness, one must first get into the core of himself at his least, for no one can know God who has not first known himself."[5] Is this not the best of all news for us who are so tormented by our weakness and imperfections? It is the knowledge of our failures that so frequently torments us into harming ourselves, yet here we are told it is the beginning of knowing God in all his greatness.

"Do you know what it means to be struck by grace?" That is theologian Paul Tillich's question, which he answers by saying: "Grace strikes us when we are in great pain and restlessness. It strikes when we walk through the dark valleys of a meaningless and empty life. It strikes when we feel our separation is deeper than usual….It strikes when our disgust for our own being, our indifference, our weakness, our hostility, and our lack of direction and composure have become intolerable to us. It strikes us when, year after year, the longed-for perfection of life does not appear."[6]

Is there any better description of the state we find ourselves in when we are most self-destructive? Is it possible that in this condition we are most ready, most well prepared for, the advent of grace? Grace is by definition the unearned, undeserved showering of favor and forgiveness raining down on the least deserving. Grace is certainly present when all is well and we sit comfortably in our easy chair, but it is never quite so evident and so over-whelmingly clear as when it greets us at the bottom of our empty garbage can, when we are hollowed out and overturned, smelling of puke and urine, kicked to the curb in some blind alley.

The conductor of the grace train calls out, "All aboard, all you who are lost and confused and have no ticket, all of you who know not where you are going, all who are hungry and thirsty, but have no money, all who are broken and bleeding but have no doc-tor, get on board...."

A Dread of Being

One of my favorite poets, Kenneth Patchen, writes:

Isn't all our dread a dread of being
Just here?
Of being only this?
Of having no other thing to become?
Of having nowhere to go really
But where we are?[7]

Perhaps the thing we fear most of all is our ordinary, pow-erless humanity. It is this powerlessness, the imperfection of our self and the realization that there is no hope of ever making it any different that is at the root of our self-destructiveness. Certain losses, critical events and specific disappointments serve to trigger this primitive awareness, but it is always there just below the surface, waiting to jump on us and drive us to self-rejection and the hatred of life.

I recently evaluated a fifty-six-year-old woman who held a loaded pistol to her head before her daughter talked her down and got police on the scene. She was distraught about her son who was dying of AIDS, drug addicted and living on the streets. He refused all help, and she was powerless against his condition. The son's condition alone would have been enough to make anyone feel sad, but it was the added weight of her powerlessness to help, her weakness in the face of her son's poverty, illness and addiction that transformed her sadness into self-destructiveness. She hated herself for not being able to save him and wanted to destroy herself for that failure.

Not only do such extreme situations force us to see our limited power, but many smaller daily events are continually uncovering our weak and helpless condition. We are in fact helpless against so much of our world: sickness, old age, death, world hunger, war, destructive weather patterns, cruel people—on and on it goes. We all, to some extent, manage to keep the awareness of our absolute powerlessness and helplessness under wraps. A party, a drink, a new suit, flirting with the secretary, dominating at sports, achieving success, watching television—all these things filter our awareness.

This is not a suggestion that it would be healthy to sit around and dwell on our flaws. It is critical that we realize and accept just who and where and what we are. It is in the lack of acceptance and awareness that we are able to fool ourselves with the illusion of perfection and control until things fall apart. Then we are suddenly in shock and panic.

John of the Cross noticed a tendency in spiritual beginners to either under- or overestimate their actual condition. He writes, "Some beginners make too little of their faults, and at other times become over-sad when they see themselves fall into them, thinking themselves to have been saints already; and thus they become angry and impatient with themselves, which is another imperfection....not realizing that if God should take their imperfections from them, they would probably become prouder and more presumptuous still."[8]

What is needed is a realistic and accurate appraisal of ourselves. This is something that is extremely hard for anyone to do. It is almost impossible for a depressed or manic person to do. To simply and accurately judge where we are with our life, what gifts and skills we have, where our growing edges lie, who loves us or who hates us, what our potential is or is not—these are all very difficult things to discern. If we can discern these things clearly, we will then be able to grow.

"If we do not fill our minds with guilt and self-recriminations, we will recognize our incompleteness as a kind of spaciousness into which we can welcome the flow of grace. We can think of our inadequacies as terrible defects, if we want, and hate ourselves. But we can also think of them affirmatively, as doorways through which the power of grace can enter our lives," writes Gerald May.[9]

There is no shame in our condition as it is. This is where we are. It is what we are. Perhaps we need some time to develop, or maybe we have been making unrealistic demands on ourselves. Others may think we are something we can never be. It is natural, unavoidable and perfect in its own way to be just as we are. However, that does not mean we cannot change or that we are going to stay there.

"The serious problems in life are never fully solved," wrote Carl Jung, and "if they should ever appear to be so, it is a sure sign that something has been lost. The meaning and purpose of a problem seems to lie not in its solution but in our working at it incessantly. This alone preserves us from stultification and petrification."[10] "Petrification" seems preferable to "this mess," but this is the secret of what Jung observes. Like John of the Cross, he sees the value in difficulty. If we could ever learn this secret, that our problems are not there to destroy us but to perfect us, we would have an entirely different approach to the fight.

Not only do we want to avoid the difficulties; we believe we will eventually figure out how to avoid them completely. Few of us would acknowledge this even to ourselves, but we secretly believe we will figure life out and get everything in order.

It may be that this one recurrent and unexamined primitive wish is at the heart of much of our despair. We believe life is, or should be, fair and free of heartache.

However, life will not be controlled, managed or figured out. This is one of the soul's special contributions. It accepts the mysterious and unmanageable aspects of self and life without panic. It relinquishes its position and finds peace and satisfaction in abandoning the fight, by letting go into what is, in faith and love.

Soul is always involved in the task of building a foundation of self-acceptance and self-love. To love and accept self and life as it is in all its imperfections is not the same as giving up all efforts at self-improvement. However, it is very much based on a commitment to self-improvement that is balanced by a realistic awareness of what is and what can be.

We will never be free of imperfection. Death will never leave us alone. This is a very freeing realization. Although it may sound a bit nihilistic, it is not negative but, rather, the foundation for all sane living. There is no reasonable way to muddle through life pretending there is no death and believing in the eventual perfection of the self without becoming quite neurotic or even psychotic. At least, we will be discouraged, depressed and haunted by the anxiety that will inevitably attend the sudden or gradual realization that we were mistaken. Avoiding and denying these realities is an essential component in becoming a sick and insane individual. Integrating and accepting them is the foundation for a sane society.

Ernest Becker, in his classic book, *The Denial of Death*, refers to all our efforts at remaining unconscious of our imperfections as "the denial of death." He insists that we deny death through this denial of our imperfections, and that in doing so we also deny life.[11] One cannot rid themselves of the reality of death and imperfection without also interfering with their ability to live.

Yet, as in all neurotic conditions, the healing of this terrific denial is contained in our capacity to face the facts head-on. Rather than deny, repress or aggress against ourselves and our human condition, our soul calls us to be who we are as we are in all our stark stupidity and weakness.

Acceptance of Being

Who in their right mind would even consider "accepting" oneself as weak, dependent, powerless and afraid? Is not the promise of popular religion, the "American way," technology, medicine and philosophy all about defeating this condition? We seem to think so. We certainly believe in some eventual state of spiritual enlightenment and intellectual or technological achievement that will ultimately do away with our imperfections and powerlessness.

Yet the truest and wisest of all spiritual traditions have always pointed us toward the acceptability of the human condition as it is rather than the promise of perfection. Jesus did not say, "Take up your best behavior, your good looking posture and all your finest deeds and follow me." He said, "Take up your cross and follow me."[12] One aspect of this "cross" is our humanity: our failures and our foolishness. Even if we were to become the most sincere and advanced believers, we would still experience no less than he did, which included being hated, betrayed and alone. Even Jesus met more people than he could ever heal, grew tired and weary, had no place to call home, experienced moments of doubt and, in his hour of greatest need, lost all conscious awareness of the Father's presence. Jesus' model for living was to remain "in the world" and the flesh with all its imperfections, but to be "not of the world" through a selfless compassion that places mercy as the highest order of business and puts our own perfection and comfort as a subordinate concern.

Kenneth Patchen, the author of the previously quoted poem, notes that our "dread of just being here" forms the basis of all dread. He knew what he was talking about when he said dread was based in our resistance to the ordinary and often unacceptable "isness" of our life. Due to polio, he was confined to a wheelchair all of his adult life. Yet he published hundreds of poems "about the things we can feel with our whole being—the senselessness of war, the need for love among men on earth, the presence of God in man, the love for a beloved woman, social justice, and the continual resurgence of the beautiful in life."[13] He never once wrote about his disability.

The secret key to the truly human path is to remain fully human when it is unpleasant to do so. Go ahead and let it hurt. The true human walks the human path knowing it is perfect that we experience imperfection. Joseph Campbell was asked if he had optimism about the world being this way, all mixed up as it is. He replied, "Yes, it's great just the way it is. And you are not going to fix it up. Nobody has ever made it any better. It is never going to be any better. This is it, so take it or leave it. You are not going to correct it or improve it."[14] He was not being cynical here, but was making the point that all religions and mythologies have been trying to teach us that this human condition must be accepted as it is. We do not transcend our state as humans by becoming perfect, but by accepting our imperfections.

Accepting ourselves as we are may be one of our primary jobs in this life. Until doing so, we will always be at odds with God, ourselves and others. There will always be this brokenness and there will always be the task to heal it through acceptance born of compassion and understanding.

CHAPTER 11
Some Practical Applications

God may be found in prayer, awareness of the "now" moment, service to others, creativity, ordinary life, nature, literature, beauty and pain. God may appear as a female or male, distant or near, silent or verbose, large or small, because God is all and in all. God is love, and will always in all ways and by all means appear wherever love can be found. He is beauty, and rises and falls within beauty's breast. God is truth and is in everything that is true and real. He may manifest as a gentle breeze or a howling tornado, as a peacock in full array or a black snake slithering through the grass.

As we open ourselves to the appearance of this grace, we must learn to be receptive, perceptive and alert to its appearance because at times it is hiding among the ordinary. The slightest gesture, even the most disturbing growl or slow moving of the moon across the horizon may hold his appearance. We must remain especially alert to relationships, intimacies, creative moments and opportunities for joy in the smallest things.

The expansion of soul will take place through the infiltration of God's love into one's life, whether that is found and cultivated through religion, art, relationships, daily living or disappointment. If we cannot find God here in the daily "now" of ordinary life we are not likely to find him anywhere.

What have others called upon at the last minute that has helped them through? It is often just one single idea. The idea of a person they love, the memory of someone or something, perhaps the hope of something yet to come. Sometimes our saving grace can be in one wise thought. Just as every skyscraper, book or amusement park begins with a single thought in the mind of its creator, so a single thought can sometimes be enough to carry us through to see the light of another day and to create a new life.

Novelist and poet Charles Bukowski has written a great deal about his suicidal thoughts and attempts. He once stuck his head in an oven, turned on the gas and lit a match. It blew up and singed his hair and eyebrows, but he was still alive, so he went downtown and got drunk.

On another occasion he writes, "I had the butcher knife against my throat one night in the kitchen." Then he remembered his daughter. "I thought, easy, old boy, your daughter may want you to take her to the zoo. Ice cream bars, chimpanzees, tigers, green and red birds, and the sun coming down on top of her head, the sun coming down and crawling into the hairs of your arms, easy, old boy."[1] That is what it takes sometimes, to remember the sacredness of everyday life, the life we have with our kids, our opportunity to see our baby laughing at the monkeys, the possibility of one more ice cream cone in the sweet summer sun. We cannot forget these things.

The poet Jane Kenyon suffered from bipolar disorder. She felt desolated, as if she belonged to the depression and was captive to it. From birth she felt the melancholy. Her depressions were so deep that suicide at times seduced her, but she said the idea that every believer is a part of the body of Christ is what kept her from harming herself. She thought by injuring herself, she was injuring the body of Christ.[2]

Can we believe we are also a part of the body and life of Christ in the world, as we most certainly are, and think again before hurting him any more? Can we remember the anguish our suicidal actions may cause in our parents or our children? Can we see how our self-destructiveness wounds the world, and take back our aggression?

In Wally Lamb's beautiful book, *She's Come Undone,* his protagonist, Delores Price, comes to her suicidal crisis after years of despair and self-hatred. She writes a suicide letter to her grandmother. She considers hanging herself. She holds a lit cigarette to her thigh and thinks of slashing her wrists with a broken drinking glass. She tries to drown herself in the ocean. Her only thought is, "I don't want to die. I don't want to live either."[3]

Knowing that she is uncertain is enough to keep her from persisting with her suicidal plans or from taking that irreversible turn. The one little awareness that she did not really want to die was enough to keep her safe, even though another part of her was insisting she should kill herself and be done with it. Staying alive with the feeling for death without acting on it is enough to bring you through to the next day. The next day will bring something new, different and, in time, something better.

Susan Rose Blauner is a woman who lived with suicidal thoughts for eighteen years and made multiple suicide attempts before she "learned how to outthink suicide." She tells how she did this in a book entitled *How I Stayed Alive When My Brain Was Trying to Kill Me.*[4] She details in her work that she "learned how to stand up to the grim reaper, refocus my thoughts, change my behavior, and make life-affirming decisions." Her book includes multiple charts, tips, lists, resource pages and more. She talks about how she finally figured out after ten years of therapy that her suicidal thinking was just a thought and that she did not have to act on that thought.

She realized too that she was "addicted" to the idea of suicide and that she could deal with it like anyone else might deal with an addiction to alcohol. She began to identify "triggers" in her environment that seemed to set off bad periods of suicidal temptation. From there she learned to make a plan for how to deal with this when it came on strong, and she prepared herself ahead of time to have an alternate response handy, to have numbers readily available for people to call, and things she could do in place of thinking of hurting herself. There are many good ideas here, and I recommend it especially for those who like worksheets and other very practical "how to" advice.

Use Reading, Writing and Reflection

One of the most interesting things Ms. Blauner did to deal with her suicidal thinking was to write her book. The process of writing and researching, reaching out to others, clarifying and refining all the dynamics involved by writing it all down was probably one of the most therapeutic things she could have done. Perhaps you could try something similar. Write a paper on "How to Battle Despair and Suicidal Thoughts," or prepare a speech you might imagine giving to a group of individuals who face the same struggles.

If you have actually worked through the experience of suicidal periods or have survived attempts, you have something to offer others. You might seek opportunities to share your story at a local school, church or mental health clinic. This may help you clarify things for yourself and will reinforce the positive things you have learned while helping others.

It may be helpful for you to make a retreat or get away from everything for some time of reflection and to build yourself back up. This is very important to consider doing and is something I frequently recommend to people who are overwhelmed but not quite in need of psychiatric hospitalization. Make yourself a cocoon. Reflect and read and pray and rest and heal. People find this difficult to do, especially when they have kids or are very conscientious about their work or responsibilities. If you are unable to do this now, you may have no other choice in another week or two, because if you "lose it" you will end up in a psychiatric ward. A resort vacation or meditation retreat is a lot cheaper than a hospital. All those things you think you have to take care of will go undone if you do not take care of yourself.

Developing a style in which you take care of your soul will have to involve a return to the realities of everyday life. You cannot hide out forever. You can learn to say no to some duties, build in little minivacations in your routine, ask for help and watch a lot of funny movies.

Remember also that God is not only found in organized religion or special meetings, but more so, he is among us in the trenches. Learning ways to be comfortable with ourselves as we are, fulfilling our mundane duties in awareness of the divine implications, remaining aware and centered throughout our day all take some practice. Soulful living is spirituality for the realist. This kind of spirituality is "seeded, germinates, sprouts and blossoms in the mundane," according to Thomas Moore.[5]

In fact, he further explains, when we are too driven to try, and instead live "fully consciously in an intellectually predictable world, protected from all mysteries and comfortable with conformity, we lose the everyday opportunities for the soulful life."[6] Soulful living is regular life lived fully, in meaningful ways, but without the fear and anxiety of trying to do it all perfectly. It is finding the nuggets of enjoyment and peace in the gaps between the flooding toilet, the carpooling and the dirty laundry. Soul enters through the little surprises, the small wonders, the sleeping cat, a call from a friend, watching the snow fall or drinking your morning tea in silence.

Inspirational and therapeutic reading is a must. All my therapy is taken from writers. A brief recommended reading list may be found at the end of this book. However, seek out classic spiritual literature, any of the mindfulness meditation-related books, the poets of your liking, the New Testament and anything on the shelves that appeals to you specifically. I strongly believe that God uses such books and that he is really good at bringing the right ones to us at the right time if we are prayerfully and mindfully receptive.

Meditation and prayer are another must. Make it your practice. Do not make this another difficult task you must learn to do well or must cram into your schedule. Make it enjoyable and do it as you can in your own way. It is meditation enough simply to be still, reflective, quiet and open. Do it for ten minutes. Do it when you are in your car. Gently and sincerely ask God to show you what you need to see and to take you where you need to go. Be attentive to the various hints and signs that will come your way.

Finding the Sacred in Ordinariness

Soul care is the practice of simple awareness. It is learning to be awake. It is being with life as it comes. It is learning to let go of the drama. It is being available to our self and to others. It is being real. It is feeling what we feel. It is making compassionate and wise choices. It is loosening our grip on our attachments, entitlements and fears. It is being here now. It is getting back up when we fall. It is being okay with not being okay. Over and again, soul care is letting ourselves love and be loved. It is allowing God to love us.

Life is sacred. Everything that supports life is sacred. Even something as miniscule and invisible as air is a sacred sustainer of the life in us. The air we breathe is a gift of God, who is the originator and sustainer of all life. Our life is a gift. The blood that is pumping through our veins keeping us alive is a gift. There are times when even an old chair can be sacred.

A friend of mine some years ago was depressed and despondent. She did not want anything to do with the things she had previously loved. She is a bit eccentric, and for some reason the only thing she wanted at this time in her life was to have an old chair refinished. It had belonged to her aunt and, for her at that time, making this connection back to her dear aunt was what she felt she needed.

Her husband thought this old chair was ready for the dump, which it was. However, her son heard what she needed to do, and he helped her in restoring the chair. My friend recovered. I cannot say the chair healed her, but it was something that helped get her through this difficult time.

A few years back I went through a period of personal darkness, probably the worst I had ever experienced. I could not get out of bed or talk. I just cried and wrote in a journal. Others were there for me. My wife stayed with me and gave me the space and reassurance I needed to work through it. Her parents let us use their condominium at the beach for a week, and we went there together, where I wrote every day, most of the day. I needed to confront God and myself as well as reconnect with myself and my wife. I talked some, but mostly, I needed to go inward, to be alone and fight with God and my inner demons. I needed time, to be quiet, not to be at work, not to have to entertain or help anyone else, to be heartbroken in my own way for a while. The condominium, the space, the support, writing, solitude, time, silence, being with the ocean were things that got me through this difficult time.

We all have to figure out what makes us tick and what keeps us from ticking. I have learned that I cannot live when I am working a job I hate, so I have tried to find things to do that I like and to go at a pace I can accept. Although this has negatively impacted my income, keeping my soul alive is more important than having a bigger house. I've learned I need to have time to be creative in order to stay alive, so I've made it a priority. I've discovered that I can't live when I am angry with God or when I think he is angry with me, so I work at our relationship. It takes a while to figure out what we need to do and what we need to refuse to do in order to keep our soul alive, and I am still trying to figure it out for myself. I think there are some practical things to which we need to pay attention so that we will begin to have an impact. The process will be something different for each of us.

Another friend, a psychologist in Danville, Virginia, told me about how she made it through a terrible period of depression brought on by divorce by working on a giant quilt. Every day she sewed and cried her way through her pain until she healed—and she had a work of art to remember her passage by.

My mother is widowed, her health has been poor and she has suffered many disappointments and losses. One of the things that keeps her going more than anything else, besides her wonderful children, is her little dog. She cooks for him, but the dog is really the one taking care of Mom. He has probably extended her life and given her a reason to get up in the morning more than anything else in her immediate environment. Many people are like that with their animals, and some have even told me they would have killed themselves if it were not for their dog or cat at home. Don't underestimate the little ordinary things of life.

Others tend a garden or build model trains. Some watch the birds. Others walk. I see these people every day, going on with their lives, lives that I am sure have at times been as hard or harder than anything you or I have had to face. They keep going because they have something to do, something about which to care. Sometimes it is something seemingly ridiculous to you or me, like the guy who used to live up the street from me in Baltimore. He had a big ongoing battle with booze, and he was winning it, one day at a time, because he had something to keep him occupied. He would wash his cars every day. Rain, shine or snow, he would be out there washing them.

Another friend of mine lives for his Harley. He drives an old rusty car and gives most of his time helping others to recover from their drug and alcohol addictions. He is not paid what he is worth, and he often gives more than what he is paid. He had to quit the drink as well and he has been through some rough times, but he lives to ride and rides to live. That Harley keeps him sane.

The suicidal person in recovery needs something to keep his soul alive. Be creative. Think about what you used to love before you were depressed. Meet some new friends. Learn to play a guitar. Get a dog.

People in recovery and therapy often talk about how we have to "fake it until we make it," meaning there are times when we have to act "as if" we are okay even before we believe it or feel it. Often the experience of being okay will follow the activity, and we cannot always wait until we feel like getting out of bed before we do it. Goethe said, "Whatever you think you can do or believe you can do, begin it. Action has magic, grace, and power in it."[7]

Other times we need some encouragement or even the permission to be okay, or perhaps some reassurance that things will work out. This is how two very saintly women in history had their lives changed, and subsequently changed the lives of many others.

St. Teresa of Avila (1515–82), who is "undoubtedly the most influential female saint in the western world," lived a life of poverty and great austerity.[8] She endured physical pain and emotional losses, and much of her spirituality and meditation centered on the way of the cross, a life of intentional self-sacrifice and mortification of the flesh. She had an experience about this, which she wrote in the following poem.

Just these two words He spoke changed my life,
  "Enjoy Me."
What a burden I thought I was to carry—a crucifix,
  as did He.

Love once said to me, "I know a song, would you like to
  hear it?"
And laughter came from every brick in the street and from
  every pore in the sky.
After a night of prayer, He changed my life when
  He sang, "Enjoy Me."[9]

Have relationships, eat your meals, toil at your labor, but
enjoy me in all of it. Stop struggling so hard to be somebody or
something you are not; stop trying to please everybody and control everything. Stop focusing all your energies on what is wrong
with the world, and just for one moment, "Enjoy me." Sometimes
I think that is all God is trying to tell us. He invites us to attend
a service in his true church, the church of love in the religion of
being happily alive.

A similar life-changing event occurred in the life of Dame
Julian of Norwich. Years of anxiety and spiritual anguish over her
sinfulness and imperfection before God were eased when she
finally heard those now famous reassuring words, "All is well and
all shall be well and all manner of things shall be well."[10] Yes, God
told her, even sin and failure have a place in my plan. Let it go,
Julian, let it go, Ken or Donna or whatever your name may be and
in whatever situation you find yourself. God says it will be all
right...you'll see.

Old chairs, a journal, a quilt, a mangy dog, a rowdy motor-
cycle. These are the kind of things some might regard as trivial,
unspiritual or common. But sometimes it is the littlest things that
give us reason to live another day.

Let Nature Teach Us

We can also learn some very practical advice on soul-full living from nature. An apple tree has never committed suicide. It does not get angry or depressed when its fruits and leaves fall to the ground and it is left standing there bare naked through the cold winter. In the summer, it is in its glory, and the red apples are glowing tastefully in the sun, the fragrance from its buds drift pleasantly through the valley and everyone comes to visit. Come winter, that all changes, and everything it previously loved about being an apple tree is gone and it can do nothing about it. Yet it refuses to give up. We might imagine it could feel disappointed and discouraged, if a tree could feel and reflect as such, but judging from what it does, we know it is never defeated. It goes on being the best apple tree it can be under any condition. It does what it can do.

The tree has been through this before, and something within it remembers how it works. Winter suggests that beauty is gone for good, but the tree "knows" that's not true. Winter tells him to give up and surrender to defeat, but he will not. This skinny little tree is not easily discouraged. This is when it stands its ground, becomes still and quiet, takes a long nap and holds on. The tree doesn't give up on life and life does not abandon it. The tree waits for and believes in spring.

The reward for all this patience and faith and wisdom is that spring does indeed return. The faith of the tree doesn't make it happen, or does it? Just when it seems things have gotten about as dark and cold as they can get and the tree begins to wonder if the ground will ever thaw, it does. Slowly, imperceptibly, the ice melts from its limbs. New shoots and sprigs arrive daily, and within a few short days the tree is returned to its glory, and the winter is forgotten.

The most amazing thing about this story is that, although we think in terms of spring as better than winter, the tree does not. Our metaphor deceives us because the tree is just as content in winter as in spring. Again, that is another deep lesson for soul to teach us.

Soul serves us best when we allow it to "know" what it knows the way a tree knows what it knows, and when we trust just the same way that the tree trusts, without attachments or aversions, simply living because we are alive. This sort of "trust" is organic; it is who we already are. We don't have to learn it as much as we have to let it, we don't have to work at it as much as we must allow it to work in us. This is beyond logic or words.

It is not in my head any more than the tree is "thinking about" blooming or making it through another winter. It is just awareness. Simply being what one is as one is in God.

CHAPTER 12
Going to God: The Soul's Journey Homeward

Hopelessness and Helplessness: The Way to God

We do not need any spiritual sophistication, intellectual integrity or physical prowess to approach God. We need no special instructions, formulations or qualifications. In fact, that gets in the way. All that is required is a brokenhearted sincerity that cries out in humility and passion. God is in the thirst as well as the quenching of the thirst, and all we need do is follow our heart's longing back to its source. Forgetting form and tradition, we must call out to God in our own way, whatever way you might call out for your mother if you were five years old and she were suddenly lost from you while traveling in a foreign country. He recognizes longing, loss and love. He is familiar with agony and despair and responds to desperation and need. He is very near to the brokenhearted.

Call to him like a house on fire. Burn with your need and emptiness and seek God as if he were your only source of water. Forget formalities and protocol. The heart is everything to God. Follow its broken cracks and flaws down into the pain and discover there your solidarity with Jesus on the cross as you call out together, "Why have you forsaken me?" knowing all the while that right there, at the worst crossroad of your life, God is working his greatest miracle. There are no rules any more than there are rules for how a drowning man is to gasp for air. He fights with all his might, single-minded, forgetting what others may think, not having the least concern for how air is "supposed to be sought" or what "air" means in any logical or scientific sense. This is do or die. No time for delay or to play games. That is how God is found. For God is not lost, we are, and when we seek the way home, we will find it.

C. S. Lewis once wrote, "I pray because I am helpless," and all true prayer must begin with such helplessness.[1] It is easy to find this beginning to prayer when we are broken because it is only in our brokenness that we truly taste our utter helplessness. Although our helplessness may just as well lead us to God when things are going good, we tend not to acknowledge our need until we are defeated, after we have experienced the insufficiency of ego. This is the opportunity and blessedness of brokenness.

When we break, our lives are directing us back to God the way a broken doll is to be referred back to its manufacturer. My daughter collects American Girl dolls. When one of their arms comes off, we do not try to glue it back together before sending it off for repair. We just send it back all mangled and torn. When it is returned to us, not only is the arm repaired, but the doll's flesh is cleaned and the hair restored. We go to God as we are, with all we have and all we lack, with all we are and are not.

The poet Rumi writes, "The way to Moses is all hopelessness and need and it is the only way to God....If you can only crawl, crawl to Him. If you cannot pray sincerely, offer your dry hypocritical, agnostic prayer; for God in His mercy accepts bad coin. If you have a hundred doubts of God, make them into ninety doubts. This is the way. Though you have broken your vows a hundred times, come again! Come again!"[2]

Once we return, we will be restored to a better condition than when we first began. Job is perhaps the world's best-known broken man. He lost everything, and his wife taunted him to suicide. Yet he refused to turn against God, even though he knew it was God who had permitted the devil to strip him down to nothing. He famously said, "Though he will kill me, yet I will trust in him...."[3] Through his ordeal he gained much, including the fact that "the LORD restored the fortunes of Job when he had prayed for his friends; and he LORD gave Job twice as much as he had before."[4] More important than having had his natural life restored, his spiritual life, that is, an intimate individual relationship with God, was initiated and made possible through his suffering. In the end he states, "I had heard of you by the hearing of the ear, but now my eye sees you."[5]

Some say "God is a crutch," as if that were a negative thing. But a crutch is a positive thing for a person with a broken leg. There is no shame in using a crutch when your leg is broken. We are all broken, underdeveloped and needy in more ways than not. No one in their right mind would consider water to be a "crutch" to a growing plant. The plant needs water and, without it, shrivels and dies. God is a necessity, whether we are broken or merely attempting to grow toward our potential as a plant. When your life is a wreck, the fire and rescue squad is not an embarrassment but a welcome relief. God is a welcome relief; he is just what we need, the answer to our questions, the fulfillment of our longing and the antidote to our despair. He is the healing balm, the light in darkness, our one true hope and only possibility in an impossible world. He is a father to the fatherless, bread to the hungry and light to those in darkness.

If you have the least spark of longing for the Absolute, you can be certain the Absolute is longing for you. No one seeks union with the One apart from this longing, and this longing comes only from the One. We are not only seeking God, but God is seeking us.

If we lack conviction, we can cry out, "Lord, I believe, but help my unbelief." If we are angry at God, confused about who he is or distraught about why he has allowed so many terrible things to happen, we must bring all that garbage to him. Yell. Cry. Spit out your despair if you must, but by any means, engage him and wrestle with him until he shows his face.

We come as we are, with all our boils and pus marks. Do not wait to be prepared or worthy, just come as you are. The invitation of God sounds like this: "Come all you who are thirsty, come to the waters; and you who have no money, come, buy, and eat! Come buy wine and milk without money and without cost. Why spend money on what is not bread, and your labor on what does not satisfy? Listen, listen to me, and eat what is good, and your soul will delight in the richest of fare. Give ear, and come to me; hear me, that your soul may live."[6]

Spending money on "what is not bread" and "what does not satisfy" is like starving and spending our last dollar on a magazine filled with pictures of gourmet breads and cakes, thinking this might give us some relief. Pictures do not satisfy; in fact, they make us more hungry. This is the picture of all human ignorance and attachment. We foolishly spend our last bit of money on worthless junk. Now we are hungry. This is when God says, come and eat, delight yourself with the richest of fare, have all you want, there is no cost.

Spiritual healing does not depend on our goodness, perfection, worthiness or understanding. We have no money to buy anything from God. Our only currency is our brokenness. "The LORD is close to the brokenhearted and saves those who are crushed in spirit," said King David.[7] Brokenness is what Jesus referred to as spiritual poverty, the precondition for entering the kingdom of God.[8] Spiritually, we are broken and impoverished, our heart is ripped apart, we have nothing left, and all we can bring is our selves just as we are in our emptiness.

This precondition for a relationship with God is as true for the beginner as it is for the veteran saint. Any one of us who attempts to pray is "lost before we begin," according to James Finley.[9] None of us likes this feeling of being lost, but we are thrown back to it time and again. The only ones Jesus found difficult to reach were the scribes and the Pharisees, the religious leaders of his day who already thought they knew how to pray and reach God. Fortunately, for the rest of us who are a bit bewildered about it all, the condition of being helpless and confused turns out to be the perfect precondition for waking up. As Meher Baba phrased it, "...the only prerequisite to waking up is total disillusionment."[10]

Faith, the Way to God

Anthony de Mello tells the story of a student who asks the master, "Is there anything I can do to make myself enlightened?" The teacher responded, "As little as you can do to make the sun rise in the morning." The questioner pressed further, "Then of what use are the spiritual exercises you prescribe?" "To make sure you are not asleep when the sun begins to arise," was the reply.[11]

There is nothing we can do to make the sun manifest its rays of sparkling warmth and illuminating clarity because it is always doing it on its own, with or without our awareness of it, with or without our help and regardless of whether we believe it is shining or not. Yet, sometimes we are too asleep to see it. Spiritual exercises are a way of paying attention to the sunrise or of waking up to the fact the sun is still there even when it is on the other side of the planet.

How aware we are of the sun's properties, how well we appreciate it and how efficiently we utilize it to grow fruits and flowers depend on how well we appropriate ourselves to it.

In Christian tradition this is called faith. To be awake when the sun begins to rise and to remember and believe that there is still a sun even when it can't be seen is the practice of faith. Some of this practice involves sharpening our awareness so that we do not miss what is already evident, and the other part is in sharpening our awareness so that we know what will appear on the horizon even before it gets there. Part of this requires some effort, or work, in order to place ourselves in the proper alignment and to open our sleepy eyes, but the sun's part is all gift and grace. We do what we can to prepare ourselves, and we watch, but then the rest is up to God.

Love, the Way to God

Love, in the end, is the Way. It is the way to God, it is God's way and it is God. It is within us and without. It is everywhere and nowhere. We can understand it, but we can never fully comprehend it. We cannot control it and it cannot control us. We can survive without it but we cannot live without it. There are no boundaries to love and no one race or nation or religious group has exclusive claim to it.

We must awaken to love if we are to awaken to ourselves and to God. There are some ways we can learn to help us awaken to love.

In the Old Testament God is often described as a torn and forsaken lover, like a faithful husband whose heart has been ripped apart by the infidelities of a straying wife. At other times he compares himself to a caring father who, after having provided protection and abundance for his children, is scorned and abandoned by them when he needs them the most. He is described as sorrowful, long-suffering, exhausted and burdened about how humanity is so repeatedly determined to self-destruct.

Rabbi Abraham Heschel, who helped me appreciate this perspective by pointing out how this "identification with the pathos of God," this emotional identification with the sorrow of God, is in some way "the central religious postulate."[12] The mythologist Joseph Campbell said something similar concerning the crucifixion of Christ. He taught that the image of a suffering God is important because it instigates compassion in humanity, and that compassion is the central relevance of any religious formulation.[13]

Biblical presentations of God's character in both the New and Old Testaments lead us to think of the creator of the universe as a person, someone who can be subject to disappointment and hurt at the hands of his creation. He weeps through his prophets. He calls for his people to turn their hearts toward him. He longs for their return. He is jealous for their affections and is sickened watching them waste their lives chasing after futile illusions and trusting in empty pleasures and false idols while he is ignored and scorned. He suffers. He waits. He is brokenhearted. He wants his children to be happy. He turns the other cheek when he is betrayed and crucified. He bleeds. He dies.

There is sorrow in him as he allows such things, but like a father who cringes every time his daughter falls from her bike, he allows such things in the hope that she will learn. He knows it is not love to force someone to remain balanced or to balance things for them or to eliminate their risk of falling. The deepest longing in God and Christ is clearly to love his creation and to be loved by them, and love guides the whole business of whatever it is that God is about. Thus the first commandment, the one that Jesus says fulfills all the others, the primary objective and most essential of all religious teachings, is to "love the Lord your God with all your heart, with all your soul, and with all your strength."[14] The first priority is not to be holy or obedient or sane, although these things are important. It is an imperative to first love, with the promise that all else will be taken care of secondary to that.

This whole love thing is an odd picture for a deity, far from what many other primitive deities have historically projected. Gods have been known to be impersonal, otherworldly, wielding power, impervious to pain. Of all the historical images of God, this Father who loves us and longs for our affection and loves in return is infinitely more appealing than any other. This God is approachable. He appeals to us most and makes the greatest sense to us, not because some philosopher was creative enough to make up an image of God that is lovable, but because this is the truth of creation and the created world. We are made in the image and likeness of God and are made to love and be loved. We know love in the way we can know God. We are destined to return to God in love and to find ourselves in that love.

Could this be possible, that all God wants is for us to love him? Is it imaginable that we are breaking God's heart every time we make choices that harm him, ourselves or his people? Could it be that God is not as distant as he seems but that his nature, the nature of love, prohibits him from getting any closer to us than we allow?

Perhaps this strange interplay between God and human persons is the only way for a true relationship between creator and creation to occur. Relationships built on love demand freedom of will. Without free will we would be servants, like the angels or the rocks, and not children. Perhaps God's self-imposed limitation in his choosing to be our "father" rather than our master is that he has restricted himself from pressing his will upon us and has opted to relate to us on an intimate interpersonal level so that the experience we may have of God can come through love. Perhaps love is the only way to make sense of what goes on or fails to go on between God and man.

Love could explain why God allows so much ambiguity, uncertainty and fragility. Fathers hurt when their children hurt, and the strongest dad will weep when his heart breaks. A father's power will not compel him to protect his children from all of life's irrationalities and accidents, but it will cause him to be available, long-suffering and comforting toward his children—no matter what.

Understanding God in this way may allow us to approach him differently, to get past our anger for his apparent absence in our lives and to forgive him for whatever he has allowed to occur in our lives, because we too have contributed to the rift.

Dante Alighieri writes, "The love of God, unutterable and perfect, flows into a pure soul the way that light rushes into a transparent object. The more love that it finds, the more it gives itself; so that, as we grow clear and open, the more complete the joy of loving is."[15]

It is important to emphasize once again how love is the answer: to make life meaningful, to recover ourselves, to overcome our despair, to refresh our souls, to rebuild meaning in life and to realize our unity with God all comes down to love. From the "deep movements of love" comes the highest form of contemplation.[16] Ursula King, speaking for the position held by most Christian mystics, in particular, Gregory of Nyssa and Dionysius, concludes, "God himself remains hidden, unknown and incomprehensible to human minds. Yet unity with God can be found through love."[17] Meister Eckhart asks the same question that has been asked throughout this book: "What keeps us alive, what allows us to endure?" He answers as we do here, "I think it is the hope of loving, or being loved."[18]

Inward longing is answered by an outward response; love calls out to love as love is in search of a lover. "Love," writes Kahlil Gibran, "gives naught but itself and takes naught but from itself.

Love possesses not nor would it be possessed; for love is sufficient unto love. Love has no other desire but to fulfill itself."[19]

The prophet of Lebanon goes on to express all that I have been trying to say in this book, that "even as love crowns you so shall he crucify you," that the path of love is a path of purgation as well as redemption, and that love, "if it finds you worthy,... threshes you to free you from your husks," and then "assigns you to his sacred fire, that you may become sacred bread for God's sacred feast."[20]

The path is clear. We know what we must do. Love more, beginning with ourselves. Allow God to love us. Ask him to forgive us for all the hurt we have caused him. Forgive him for whatever we have been holding against him. Go to him, like a lost child. Seek him out like an estranged lover. Love him.

The more we love, the more he allows our hearts to be filled with the "unutterable and perfect" love of himself, and as he fills us we find the capacity to love all the more. Love, then, is the light, the dispelling of the darkness from which we suffer, illuminating and transforming every darkened corner of our lives.

We may very well find ourselves again backed into other dark corners and crevices. We may need to be filled with the light all over again, but this is the hope and the beauty of God's love. It is made new and fresh every instant, it never goes dull or dim, it is never exhausted and cannot ever possibly refuse to flow into any darkened space in the soul that loves.

God is our greatest longing, and the fulfillment of that longing. All human longings, efforts and desires are poorly defined and haphazardly executed substitute longings for our primary longing for God, for the love that is both the foundation for and manifestation of the One from which we have wandered. What we seek to find in human relationships, pleasures, achievements and beauty is in the face of God, and all that we can find in God's face will be reflected back in the faces of others and our selves who cry out for more of the love that is already loving us in God.

When all is said and done, the love in us that has been awakened by God through our suffering is God himself in us loving us and longing for love. The love of God is unutterable, unimaginable and beyond anything we can attain in our self, yet it is right here within us, calling out for more of God, longing for God and pulling us ever gently into deeper revelations of God's perfect self manifest in love. Right now there is nothing you can do to make God love you more perfectly. Right now, there is nothing you have done or will ever do that will cause God to love you any less perfectly.

James Finley writes, "This is what Christ came to reveal; that nothing is missing anywhere. Our very life is the manifestation of the union with God we seek. And so in the end we learn to extend the compassionate love of Christ to ourselves in our inability to realize how invincibly precious and one with God we are in all our wayward ways."[21]

Let the love in you reclaim your self and reunite you to God, then go about doing good for others. I don't think the suicidal darkness will be able to find you there if you go there with all your mind, heart and soul.

Notes

INTRODUCTION: Before the Flooding Brink

1. Shawn Christopher Shea, *The Practical Art of Suicide Prevention* (Hoboken, NJ: John Wiley and Sons, 2002), 9.

2. Susan Rose Blauner, *How I Stayed Alive When My Brain Was Trying to Kill Me* (New York: William Morrow, 2002), 225.

3. Ibid.

4. See Matthew 16:26.

CHAPTER 1: Darkness in the Heart

1. See Galatians 5:22, 23.

2. Edward Hoagland, quoted in Debexena.com.

3. Chuck Palahniuk, *Fight Club* (New York: Henry Holt, 1996).

CHAPTER 2: Wounded Innocence

1. Julian of Norwich, *Revelations and Motherhood of God*, trans. Francis Beer (Cambridge: D. S. Brewer, 1998), 37, 38.

2. John 3:17.

3. Matthew 18:21–22.

4. John 3:19.

CHAPTER 3: Can a Suicide Be Prevented?

1. Susan Rose Blauner, *How I Stayed Alive When My Brain Was Trying to Kill Me* (New York: William Morrow, 2002), 5.

2. Gerald May, *Will and Spirit: A Contemplative Psychology* (New York: Harper and Row, 1987), 5.

3. Ibid., 6.

4. Nicholas of Cusa, in Lorraine Kisly, *Christian Teachings on the Practice of Prayer* (Boston and London: New Seeds, 2006), 6.

5. Lao Tzu, *The Way of Life*, trans. Witter Bynner (New York: Perigee Books, 1944, 1972), 49.

6. Francis of Assisi, in Christian Bobin, *The Secret of Francis of Assisi: A Meditation* (Boston and London: Shambhala, 1999), 53.

7. William James, in Lou Marinoff, *Therapy for the Sane*, (New York and Bloomsbury, 2004), vii.

CHAPTER 4: Understanding the Suicidal Condition

1. Ernest Hemingway, in A. E. Hotchner, *Papa Hemingway* (New York: Bantam, 1966), 246.

2. Greg Hemingway, *Papa: A Personal Memoir* (New York: Penguin, 1977), 136.

3. Hotchner, 328.

4. Greg Hemingway, 34.

5. Hotchner, 331.

6. Hotchner, 323.

7. Greg Hemingway, 24.

8. Lorraine Kisly, *Christian Teachings on the Practice of Prayer* (New York and Boston: New Seeds, 2006), 51.

9. Meister Eckhart, *Meister Eckhart: A Modern Translation*, trans. Raymond Blakney (New York: Harper Torchbooks, 1941), 41.

10. See Elio Frattaroli's *Healing the Soul in the Age of the Brain* as a good example (New York: Viking/ Penguin, 2001).

11. Thomas Moore, *Care of the Soul* (New York: HarperCollins, 1994), 146.

12. Erich Fromm, *Man for Himself* (Greenwich, CT: Fawcett, 1970), 218.

13. St. John of Kanty, in Jane Cavolina and Matthew Bunson, eds., *All Shall Be Well: Hope and Inspiration from Great Catholic Thinkers* (New York: Berkley, 2004), 93.

14. Romans 7:24, 25.

15. See James 1:2–5.

16. Fredrick Buechner in *Spiritual Quests: The Art and Craft of Religious Writing* (New York: Quality Paperback Book Club, 1988), 111.

CHAPTER 5: The Promise of Soul

1. Thomas Aquinas, in Daniel Ladinsky, ed., *Love Poems from God: Twelve Sacred Voices from the East and West* (New York: Penguin Compass, 2002), 132.

2. Teresa of Avila, ibid., 275.

3. Francis de Sales, in Ursula King, *Christian Mystics* (Mahwah, NJ: Paulist Press, Hidden Spring, 2001), 160.

4. 2 Corinthians 4:8–9.

5. Galatians 5: 22–23.

6. Thomas Merton, *No Man Is an Island* (New York: Barnes and Noble Books, 2002), 125.

7. Jean-Pierre de Caussaude, *Abandonment to Divine Providence* (New York: Doubleday, Image, 1975), 46.

8. Ibid., 61, 64.

9. Brother Lawrence, in *Christian Classics in Modern English*, ed. Bernard Bangley (Wheaton, IL: Harold Shaw Publishers, 1986), 29.

10. Tim Farrington, ed. *Cloud of Unknowing* (New York: HarperCollins Spiritual Classics, reprinted from Paulist Press version, 1981), 31.

11. James Finley, *Christian Meditation: Experiencing the Presence of God* (New York and San Francisco: HarperCollins, 2004).

CHAPTER 6: Damage Control

1. Edwin Shneidman, *The Suicidal Mind* (New York and Oxford: Oxford University Press, 1996), 166.

2. Isaiah 40:31.

3. Psalm 46:10.

4. Joseph Campbell, with Bill Moyers, *The Power of Myth* (New York: Doubleday, 1988), 119.

CHAPTER 7: The Role of Adversity

1. Paul Evodokimov, in Lorraine Kisly, *Christian Teachings on the Practice of Prayer* (Boston and London: New Seeds, 2002), 30.

2. Matthew 5:3–10.

3. Thomas Moore, *Care of the Soul* (New York: Harper-Collins, 1992); see chapter 7.

4. St. John of the Cross, *Dark Night of the Soul* (Mineola, NY: Dover Thrift Edition, 2003), 7.

5. John Keats in *The Norton Anthology of English Literature*, ed. M.H. Abrams (New York: W. W. Norton, 1975), 1904.

6. Ken Stifler, *Approaching the Speed of Light* (Baltimore: True Vine Publications, 1986), 19.

7. Stephen Batchelor, *Verses from the Center* (New York: Riverhead Books, 2000), 21.

CHAPTER 8: Live the Questions

1. R. M. Rilke, in Jane Cavolina and Matthew Bunson, eds., *All Shall Be Well: Hope and Inspiration from Great Catholic Thinkers* (New York: Berkley, 2004), 82.

2. Paulo Coelho, *The Fifth Mountain* (New York: HarperCollins, 1998), 212.

3. Psalm 107: 4–43.

4. Anthony Bloom, *Beginning to Pray* (Mahwah, NJ: Paulist Press, 1970), xvii.

5. Gregory of Nyssa, in Ernest Kurtz and Katherine Ketcham, eds., *The Spirituality of Imperfection* (New York: Bantam Books, 1992), 30.

6. Meister Eckhart, in Joseph Campbell, with Bill Moyers, *The Power of Myth* (New York: Doubleday, 1988), 49.

7. Paul Tillich, *The Courage to Be* (New Haven and London: Yale University Press, 1952), 190.

8. Viktor Frankl, *Man's Search for Ultimate Meaning* (New York: MJF Books, 2000), 133.

9. Thomas Merton, *No Man Is an Island* (New York: Barnes and Noble Books, 2003), 77, 80, 84.

10. Ibid., 183.

11. Jack Kornfield, *A Path with Heart* (New York: Bantam New Age Books, 1993), 73.

12. James 1:2–4.

CHAPTER 9: Soul Recovery: The Secret Center of the World

1. Juan Ramon Jimenez, in Kate Farrell, ed., *Art and Wonder* (New York: The Metropolitan Museum of Art and Bulfinch Press, 1996), 45.

2. Robert Bly, *Iron John* (Reading, MA, Menlo Park, CA, and New York: Addison Wesley, 1990), 123.

3. Thomas Moore, *Care of the Soul* (New York: HarperCollins, 1992), 20.

4. Caroline Myss, *Sacred Contracts* (New York: Harmony Books, 2001), 138.

5. James Hillman, *The Soul's Code: In Search of Character and Calling* (New York: Random House, 1996). See book as a whole.

6. Moore, 19.

7. Antoine De St.-Exupery, in Jane Cavolina and Matthew Bunson, eds., *All Shall Be Well: Hope and Inspiration from Great Catholic Thinkers* (New York: Berkley, 2004), 77.

8. Moore, 12.

9. James 4:6.

10. James 4:8.

CHAPTER 10: Loving Yourself

1. Thomas Merton, *The New Man* (New York: Farrar, Straus and Giroux, 1999), 233.

2. Bruce Springsteen, *Songs* (New York: HarperCollins, 2003), 297.

3. Thomas Merton, *No Man Is an Island* (New York: Barnes and Noble Books, 2003), 129.

4. Thérèse of Lisieux, in John Beevers, trans., *The Autobiography of Saint Thérèse of Lisieux: The Story of a Soul* (New York: Doubleday, 2001), 129.

5. Meister Eckhart, in Raymond Blakney, trans., *Meister Eckhart: A Modern Translation* (New York: Harper and Row, 1941), 246.

6. Paul Tillich, *The Shaking of the Foundations* (New York: Charles Scribner's Sons, 1948), 161, 162.

7. Kenneth Patchen, *Selected Poems* (New York: New Directions, 1957), 48.

8. St. John of the Cross, *Dark Night of the Soul* (Mineola, NY: Dover Thrift Edition, 2003), 7.

9. Gerald May, *Addiction and Grace* (New York: HarperCollins, 1991), 31.

10. Carl Jung, in John Welch, *Spiritual Pilgrims: Carl Jung and Teresa of Avila* (New York and Mahwah, NJ: Paulist Press, 1982), 94.

11. Ernest Becker, *The Denial of Death* (New York: Simon and Schuster, 1997).

12. Matthew 16:24.

13. Kenneth Patchen, *Selected Poems* (New York: New Directions, 1957), back cover.

14. Joseph Campbell, with Bill Moyers, *The Power of Myth* (New York: Doubleday, 1988), 65.

CHAPTER 11: Some Practical Applications

1. Charles Bukowski, *Post Office* (Santa Rosa, CA: Black Sparrow Press, 2002), 192.

2. Jane Kenyon on her bipolar disorder.

3. Wally Lamb, *She's Come Undone* (New York: Pocket Books, 1992), 247.

4. Susan Rose Blauner, *How I Stayed Alive When My Brain Was Trying to Kill Me* (New York: William Morrow, 2002), 43.

5. Thomas Moore, *Care of the Soul* (New York: Harper-Collins, 1992), 233.

6. Ibid., 233.

7. Goethe, in Julia Cameron, *The Artist's Way* (New York: Jeremy P. Tarcher/Putnam, 1992), 67.

8. Daniel Ladinsky, ed., *Love Poems from God: Twelve Sacred Voices from the East and West* (New York: Penguin Compass, 2002), 268.

9. Teresa of Avila, ibid., 276.

10. Julian of Norwich, in Jane Cavolina and Matthew Bunson, eds., *All Shall Be Well: Hope and Inspiration from Great Catholic Thinkers* (New York: Berkley, 2004), 61.

CHAPTER 12: Going to God: The Soul's Journey Homeward

1. C. S. Lewis, in Jane Cavolina and Matthew Bunson, eds., *All Shall Be Well: Hope and Inspiration from Great Catholic Thinkers* (New York: Berkley, 2004), 119.

2. Rumi, in Kabir Helminski, ed., *The Rumi Collection* (Boston and London: Shambhala, 2000), 94, 95.

3. Job 13:15 (footnoted alternate version).

4. Job 42:10.

5. Job 42:5.

6. Isaiah 55:1–3.

7. Psalm 34:18.

8. See Matthew 5: 4, 5.

9. James Finley, *Merton's Place of Nowhere* (Notre Dame, IN: Ave Maria Press, 1978), 12.

10. Attributed to Meher Baba by Deepak Chopra, exact reference unknown.

11. Anthony de Mello, *One Minute Wisdom* (New York: Doubleday, 1985), 11.

12. Abraham J. Heschel: my thanks for this perspective brought to life in his book, *The Prophets* (New York: Harper Torchbooks, 1969).

13. Joseph Cambell, *Myths To Live By* (New York: The Viking Press, 1972), 153.

14. Matthew 22:37.

15. Dante Alighieri, in Kate Farrell, ed., *Art and Wonder,* (New York: Metropolitan Museum of Art and Bulfinch Press, 1996), 129.

16. Ursula King, *Christian Mystics* (Mahwah, NJ: Paulist Press, Hiddenspring, 2001), 229.

17. Ibid., 196.

18. Meister Eckhart, in Daniel Ladinsky, *Love Poems from God: Twelve Sacred Voices from the East and West* (New York: Penguin Compass, 2002), 109.

19. Kahlil Gibran, *The Prophet* (New York: Alfred A. Knoff, 1958), 11–13.

20. Ibid.

21. James Finley, *Christian Meditation: Experiencing the Presence of God* (New York and San Francisco: HarperCollins, 2004), 126.

Suggested Resources

This book is based on the belief that grace wants us to be happy, loving and creatively alive. It also assumes that, although we cannot control grace, we *can* determine how much of this grace we experience at any given moment. This is accomplished through faith, which is to say it is determined by what we believe and how we think. Beliefs are thought choices, and although some seriously suicidal or despairing individuals may initially need a little medication or supervision in order to make it through a dangerous time, ultimately the power to change and heal is in us. This is God's power in us, the power of life and of love. These gifts are already in us, and no one is without them. Reading can help you find them and call them forth.

Here are a few ideas. This is a very abbreviated list, so I also encourage you to go to your local bookstore or library and browse. Search for anything positive and inspirational. There is almost no limit to the amount of psychological help you can get from therapeutic reading:

Cavolina, Jane, and Matthew Bunson. *All Shall Be Well: Hope and Inspiration from Great Catholic Thinkers.* New York: Berkley, 2004. Well-selected positive quotes from Blaise Pascal, Ignatius Loyola, Hildegard von Bingen, Mother Teresa, Francis of Assisi, Graham Greene and many others.

de Cassaude, Jean-Pierre. *Abandonment to Divine Providence.* New York: Doubleday, Image, 1975. I mention this as perhaps the most powerful and transformative book in the genre of classic Christian literature. I personally believe if one could practice de Caussaude's instructions they would never be depressed, discouraged or self-absorbed.

Finley, James. *Christian Meditation: Experiencing the Presence of God.* New York and San Francisco: HarperCollins, 2004. The subtitle of this awesome book is a better description of its contents than is the main. The chapter "The Self-Transforming Journey" is worth the price, but you also get thirteen other chapters describing not only "how to" meditate but, more important, what it is to be whole in our brokenness through the realization that we are already being loved into being.

Goldstein, Joseph. *Insight Meditation: The Practice of Freedom.* Boston: Shambhala, 1993. This book is included as a recommended introductory text for anyone interested in the field of mindfulness training or Buddhist psychology. There is an incredible wealth of healing information in this area, and many find their way to healing and wholeness through practicing or studying any number of the world's mystical traditions.

Huxley, Aldous. *The Perennial Philosophy.* New York: Harper and Row, 1944, 1945. An absolute, "must have" classic demonstrating the singular beauty of all mystics, East and West, as they speak of the universal love and Being that participates in the world, making all things right.

Kurtz, Ernest, and Katherine Ketcham. *The Spirituality of Imperfection.* New York: Bantam Books, 1992. Full of sage advice on how to accept ourselves and our world even though both are filled with the failures, limitations and imperfections we find so hard to accept.

May, Gerald. *Will and Spirit: A Contemplative Psychology*. New York: Harper and Row, 1982. This is one of those books that should have transformed the field of psychology the way Carl Rogers or Albert Ellis did, but, for some reason, it failed to have the broad appeal it deserved. I recommend it for anyone working toward their own sense of how to integrate spiritual and psychological approaches to human problems, be it their own or that of the people they work with.

Merton, Thomas. *No Man Is an Island*. New York: Barnes and Noble Books, 2003. Read Merton. Begin with this one. It offers thoughts on recovering the "possession of our own being" in order to experience "God Himself accomplishing in us the things we find impossible" (pp. 123, 127). Merton has a strong devotion to the notion of God's love in us being the path to our true self, accomplishing in us our fullest human potential and being. At times you have to read around Merton's traditional Catholic language in order to appreciate the gems of his profound existential philosophy.

Osbon, Diane K., ed. *Reflections on the Art of Living: A Joseph Campbell Companion*. New York: HarperCollins, 1991. This is perhaps the best place to begin enjoying the wisdom of Joseph Campbell. It's hard to beat his discussions about how to "live out of one's own center" in order to "remain radiant in the filth of the world" (pp. 73, 189).

Ruiz, Dom Miguel. *The Four Agreements*. San Rafael, CA: Amber-Allen Publishing, 1997. This has been a life-changing book for some people. One of the best things it teaches and inspires one to learn is how to remain unaffected by other people's drama. If you are often overwhelmed by other people's negativity, you might like this one.

Schumacher, E. F. *A Guide for the Perplexed.* New York: Harper and Row, 1977. This small classic is a brief but powerful introduction to positive philosophy, offering what Theodore Roszak called "a harvest of utterly sane, consoling, and life-affirming insight from one of the wisest minds of our time."

Tolle, Eckhart. *The Power of Now.* Novato, CA: New World Library, 1999. This book seems to consolidate and update the best of what hundreds of other similar books have attempted to say about being present and aware and alive through conscious awareness, yet does a better job of making it seem practical and obtainable.

Other Resources for Suicidal Persons and Their Families

Crisis Hotlines:
1. Call 911 in your local area for immediate response from local police who can intervene and get you or someone you love to a safe place of assessment and/or treatment. Know that there are laws in place in every state that allow law enforcement authorities to intervene even if the suicidal person is unwilling or unable to participate voluntarily.
2. National Hopeline Network: 1-800-SUICIDE (1-800-784-2433)
3. Covenant House Nineline: 1-800-999-9999
4. Girls and Boys Town National Hotline: 1-800-850-8076

Organizations:
1. American Association of Suicidology: www.suicide.org or 4201 Connecticut Ave. NW, Suite 408, Washington, DC 20008. Phone: 202-237-2280 (not a hotline).
2. American Foundation for Suicide Prevention: www.afsp.org or 120 Wall St., 22nd Floor, New York, NY 10005. Phone: 1-888-333-AFSP (not a hotline).
3. Suicide Information and Education Center: www.suicide info.ca. Web site with a database of information related to suicidal behaviors, prevention, intervention and follow-up for survivors.